"I DON'T KNOW WHAT TO SAY . . .'

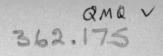

Also by Dr Robert Buckman

What You Need to Know About Cancer

"I DON'T KNOW WHAT TO SAY . . ."

How to Help and Support Someone Who Is Dying

BY DR ROBERT BUCKMAN

WITH CONTRIBUTIONS BY
Ruth Gallop, R.N., and Rev. John Martin

PAN BOOKS

First published 1988 by Macmillan and Papermac

This edition published 1996 by Pan Books
an imprint of Macmillan Publishers Ltd
25 Eccleston Place, London SW1W 9NF
and Basingstoke

Associated companies throughout the world

ISBN 0 330 34754 3

Copyright © Dr Robert Buckman 1988

The right of Dr Robert Buckman to be identified as the
author of this work has been asserted by him in accordance
with the Copyright, Designs and Patents Act 1988.

9 8 7 6 5 4 3 2

A CIP catalogue record for this book is available from
the British Library.

Printed and bound in Great Britain

Contents

Preface   ix
Author's Note   xi
Introduction   3

I *Talking and Listening*

1 Why Talk? Why Listen?   15
2 Sensitive Listening   20
3 Why You Need to Know What's Going On   31

II *The Process of Dying*

4 The Transition   37
5 Facing the Threat   42
6 Being Ill   91
7 The Last Stage   108
8 Saying Good-bye: The Function of Grief   132
9 Spiritual Aspects   145

III *Practicalities*

10 Things Every Caregiver Should Do   159
11 Individual Relationships   164

12   AIDS and Dementing Diseases   214
13   Talking with Health Professionals   223
     Conclusion   227

     Appendix A   The Living Will   229
     Appendix B   Supporting Organizations   231
     Recommended Reading   235
     Index   237

Preface

In writing this book I have drawn on the skills and expertise of two people — Ruth Gallop and John Martin. We wrote it together, not just because we share a professional involvement with terminally ill people, but also because of our respective backgrounds. John Martin is a chaplain with wide experience in street ministry. He spent several years helping people on the fringes of society before he focused on the care of the terminally ill and took up his present post as hospital chaplain at the cancer center where I work. Ruth Gallop has trained both as a nurse and as a psychotherapist, but her experience goes far beyond her training. Her first husband, Leslie, died before his thirtieth birthday, of a rare tumor after two years of illness, leaving her with a young son. When that happened, over fifteen years ago, I was a medical student, and the many conversations I had with both Ruth and Leslie changed my view of medicine. It is largely as a result of what I learned from them that I decided to specialize in cancer medicine. Ruth has brought to this book the insights of a talented psychotherapist and of someone who has been through the experience of a deep loss. She survived that loss, rebuilt her family and her life, and has achieved remarkable personal and professional growth as a result. My personal experience was with an autoimmune disease (in which the body's defense system overreacts and attacks the body itself) which nearly paralyzed me for two years and at one stage threatened my life. It taught me many things that I should have known before. As a patient I learned the value of the sympathy and support that distinguishes good doctors from ordinary ones.

Many other people have helped me, directly and indirectly. Dr. Eve Wiltshaw showed me that a doctor can be both expert and humane. Robin and Prue Skynner taught me the central elements of therapeutic dialogue. Reverend Robert Hunt helped me with many aspects of ethical and spiritual issues.

In putting this book together, we have tried to use as much as we could of what we have learned from our patients and their families. Supporting someone who is dying is always demanding and often exhausting, but it is one of the most worthwhile things that one human being can do for another. For everyone who takes on this important job, I hope that *"I Don't Know What to Say . . ."* will be of real and practical help.

"I Don't Know What to Say..."

⌘ "I'm very grateful for Robert Buckman's book. It deals, with honesty, love and deep practicality, with a subject that the vast majority of people prefer to pretend does not exist. But death is a fact of life and it is one with which we must all come to terms. With Dr Buckman's help readers can come to terms not only with the death of people they care about but with their own eventual deaths. And that is something for which, as I say, I personally am very grateful."

Claire Rayner

"There is much to receive as well as to give in being with those who are dying or bereaved. Here is a book to help us meet in this demanding and rewarding area of communication and, indeed, at many other times. Its ease of style and clarity of presentation will help many, both among the general public and professionals. We are all in Dr Buckman's debt once again."

Dame Cicely Saunders, DBE, FRCP, FRCS

'Most useful and compassionate."

Jack Jones

Who Is "the Patient"? Who Is "the Friend"? — A Note about Word Usage

Throughout this book I use the word "patient" to mean "the person who has the illness." It's unfortunate that there isn't a better word, because "patient" is a word with overtones of hospitals and doctors, and it does sound rather clinical. But it's the best word we've got at the moment. Recently some authors have started talking about persons with cancer as PWCs, which sounds even more clinical and less personal, and is a thoroughly backward step.

When I use the word "patient" I never forget that every patient is a person, and that all patients are persons before they become ill, during their illness, and afterward in our minds and memories. In my view there is a central formula:

patient = person + disease

Even though "patient" is much colder than the real people it describes, it's simply the best word we have.

Similarly, I shall use "friend" to describe anyone in the support circle of the patient — whether spouse, parent, child, sibling, close friend, or colleague.

I'm also going to avoid constant repetition of "he or she" and "him or her" by alternating the gender of the personal pronouns throughout the text. These are simply ways of making the book easier to read.

Introduction

I bumped into James in the lobby of the hospital. I was a junior medical student and my family and his had been friends for as long as I could remember. James's mother had recently been admitted to the hospital. She was found to have cancer of the kidney. James was sitting downstairs in the lobby looking miserable and blank. I asked him whether he was on his way up to see his mother. "I've been sitting here for half an hour," he said. "I want to go and see her, but I'm stuck. I don't know what to say."

As I sat with him, I realized that if it had been my mother upstairs in the hospital bed, I wouldn't have known what to say either. And as I went on through medical school and into medical practice I realized that thousands of people don't know what to say — and that includes some doctors. Most of us don't know what to say because nobody has told us. I decided to write this book for James, for myself, and for everybody else who wants to but doesn't know how to help a friend or relative facing the end of his life.

I've written this book with two purposes in mind: first, to explain the process of dying and death in enough detail to demystify it for friends or family members of the dying person, and second, to give practical advice to those close to the dying person who want to help. I'm going to explain in plain English what goes wrong so often between patient and family. I'll show how misunderstandings and obstacles arise, and how they can be dealt with — or at least how the problems created can be minimized. Reading this book will help you understand the often complex emotions that you may be feeling, as well as the equally complex emotions of the dying person. You'll find that there are many different ways to sidestep the blocks and bridge the communication gaps.

This book will help you understand what's going on and how you can help. It won't abolish the pain and the difficulty, but it will make them easier to bear. In that respect, it's similar to a book on pregnancy and childbirth: the more you know about what's happening and what's likely to happen, the less anxious and frightened you are — but no book can shorten a pregnancy or make a birth totally painless.

In some ways, the Big Secret is simply that there's no Big Secret. All that is needed is a desire to help and an understanding of what's going on. I assume that you're reading this book because you have that desire, and I hope the book will give you the understanding. This book will also give you permission — permission to feel the way you do feel, to say the things that need to be said, and to help and support the patient in the way you really want. If the image of James feeling nervous and "stuck" because he didn't know what to say to his mother strikes a chord with you, then the first thing you need to know is that you're not alone. Most people don't know how to help, not because of their own failings or inadequacies but because serious illness and the threat of death are powerful forces indeed. They can — and often do — tear relationships apart, separating and isolating the patient from family and friends while creating confusion and embarrassment. As a doctor specializing in cancer medicine, as a family member, and to a limited extent as a patient, I've seen hundreds of marriages, relationships, and friendships split apart by illness and death. But more importantly, I've seen how things can often be made better in relatively easy ways.

While nothing you read here can take away the pain of losing your friend — only the completion of grief will do that — you may be able to understand better the emotions and the reactions experienced by both you and the patient. A greater understanding will help you deal with the confusion and the awkward silences and the subtle resentments that might otherwise get in the way.

I should indicate here that I have no personal belief in the mystique of death. I don't see death as a fine and wonderful thing in itself. I don't see it as a white light, a secret garden, a butterfly coming out of a cocoon, or any other evocative image, however beautiful. Some people who have strong images like these gain an inner peace and tranquility that allows them to accept dying with little difficulty. But for many people that kind of inner support does not exist; they need the kind of support you can provide with the help of this book.

To me, dying is merely the end of a life. It is almost always sad, even though the end to much physical suffering may come as a natural relief. You won't, then, find a magic formula in this book to ease your pain miraculously and convert the loss of your friend into a joyous transition. There are no instant solutions. Instead, I have tried to identify the most important questions and to offer ways of arriving at solutions that will help you and your friend.

Why Talking about Dying Is Difficult

Our society has decided that dying is not part of the business of living. Phrases describing dying as "the last taboo" or "the new obscenity" may be clichés, but they do tell us something about the way we think. They tell us that we think of death as something alien, something outside the bounds of daily life, something unnatural. We all readily admit that death is not unnatural. We acknowledge that all life ends in death and that (another cliché) death is the one thing of which we can all be absolutely certain. We know this in our minds, but as a society we've decided not to acknowledge it, not to talk about it in a natural way. Instead, we pretend that it isn't really there.

So what? Why should we acknowledge death?

When a person is dying, his friends and family can no longer deny the reality of death. But if they have not previously acknowledged its existence, they will be ill prepared to face it. The denial of death creates a barrier between the dying person and the rest of society; the person facing death seems to have stepped outside the boundaries of our society before he has taken leave of life. He becomes isolated, set apart from his friends by the conventions of society at the very time that he most needs our support. One patient of mine, Dora, said that talking about dying simply wasn't "the done thing." She felt that this sort of conversation broke fundamental rules of what was permissible — rules accepted by her family and by "everyone." It took a lot of discussion before Dora came to realize (with great relief) that talking about dying *would not* break any laws or violate any taboos.

Why has dying become isolated from our daily life? The major causes seem to be these:

- our elders rarely die at home
- we have very high expectations of health and life
- our society places a high emphasis on material values
- there is currently a crisis in spiritual direction

I am not condemning these things as necessarily wrong. I don't believe that our society is now self-destructive and evil, nor do I believe that everything was wonderful and perfect a century ago. The fact is, however, that the way we currently lead our daily lives in Western society makes confronting death with equanimity very difficult.

Let me start with the way in which death is excluded from most people's experience of growing up. Only a few decades ago, when the extended family was more common, when grandparents would live in the same home as their grandchildren, elderly relatives often died at home surrounded by their family. As a result young children were likely to have their first experience of a death when they were quite young, and, more importantly, surrounded by people close to them. In other words, dying was seen by these younger children as a natural part of family living. Sometimes the elderly relative did not gently fade away, surrounded by the nearest and dearest. But pain and trauma would occur inside the supportive family circle, so that however unpleasant, death was still a natural part of growing up. Today most adults have not seen anyone die

at home. To them, death may appear to be foreign and
unknown.

A second reason dying has been set apart from everyday
experience is that we now have a greater expectation of a
healthy life. Every time the newspapers carry stories of a
major breakthrough in medicine — whether it's a heart
transplant, marrow grafting, Interleukin-2, or anything
else — our attitudes to illness and death change further.
Each time we tend to think, "Fine, they've fixed that, what
next?" At the back of our minds, perhaps, we're hoping
that "they" are going to come up with a cure for old age —
and preferably before we get old ourselves. This attitude
isn't a bad thing in itself. We should greet advances in
health care positively, even though many of the most
public advances may affect only a few people and may not
prolong the average life expectancy at all. But each time we
see the frontiers of health pushed forward a little bit, each
time we hear that a previously incurable disease is now
treatable, we start to hope that a cure for everything lies
just around the corner. In other words, we move closer to
thinking of death as something that can be prevented
forever with just another little bit of technical know-how.
Of course, we know that there's no such thing as immortality. But as our expectations of a healthy life increase,
the thought of dying becomes even more alien and more
unnatural.

Third, illness and dying seem to have become the province of experts. That, too, is quite logical. Looking after
sick people is often a business that requires the technical
knowledge housed in hospitals full of expensive equipment
and drugs. Naturally, if it takes high-tech medicine, equipment, and expertise to make someone even temporarily

better, then that person should be in a high-tech environment. This situation rarely creates major difficulties while the patient is getting better. But serious problems can arise when she is no longer improving and begins the process of dying. In a high-tech curing phase, family and friends seem to have little role to play in supporting her, and the illness becomes the exclusive business of the hospital and the doctors. But when medical technology has nothing further to offer, the friends may feel they have already lost their role and so remain at a distance, expecting more intervention from the doctors.

If the doctors were as good at caring for dying patients as they are at looking after acute illnesses, there would be no problem. They would feel comfortable handing back some of the support of the dying person to the family. However, doctors are often reluctant to accept the failure of their techniques. Thus, at the time when friends and family could be of greatest value to the patient, doctors feel uneasy about admitting to a newly limited role. Inadvertently, the medical staff may become a dog in the manger, unable to support the patient but equally unable to hand over to those who could.

None of this is intended as destructive criticism of the medical profession. As doctors, we do our best to be experts in treating patients, and it is unfortunate that most of us have not been taught the additional skills required to support patients suffering from incurable diseases. Now, however, these skills are included in the curriculum of many medical schools. It is likely that the next generation of doctors will be much more expert in relieving the symptoms of dying patients, and in involving the family and friends in their support. For now, however, the fact that many patients are under the medical care of experts un-trained in the nuances of care at the end of life is further reason for death to appear as an alien and unusual event.

Other reasons for our thinking of death as outside the normal business of life involve the way our society values the various aspects of our lives. An acquisitive society at-taches tremendous importance to material values and suc-cess, however temporary. The worth and meaning of a life are usually assessed in material terms. Materialism is not intrinsically wrong or dangerous, but it has a price: the more a society accepts material values as the standard by which a life is assessed, the more that society will under-value human contacts and interrelationships, and the more it will regard the end of life as fearsome and tragic. For materialistic people life is fun; death is the end of fun.

A further social cause of the estrangement of death from life is the way in which spiritual values and religion have changed. Back when there was little knowledge of the workings of the physical universe, it was easy to con-jure up a strong image of God as a divine architect who controlled all events on earth and who would mete out rewards after death. As more and more knowledge accumulated about physical events previously considered eternal mysteries, the perception of the role and the realm of God and religion have changed. Some religions now focus on personal faith. Others have tried to retain older traditions and the values that went with them. As a result of these changes, many patients are not accustomed to strong spiritual influences in their daily lives. They can-not, therefore, call on a lifelong faith to support them at the end.

These, then, are some of the most important social fac-tors that make the subject of death difficult to talk about.

But this materialistic summation of a life makes it easy to lose sight of a simple truth: death ends life but certainly doesn't rob it of meaning. We all need to remember that in our lives we affect and change the people closest to us. Those changes have a considerable value. For instance, I am not the same person that I would have been if I had not met James, Ruth, John, or the many others who have made a lasting impression on me. Some people even think of these changes as a form of immortality. They suggest that people who have died, or who are dying, do live on, in the changes they have caused in those who survive them. Having a library or an office block named after you cannot make people remember you. But if you've altered the way people think, then some of the meaning of your life will go on after your death.

Society, then, for a number of reasons views death as something outside the mainstream of life. As a result, we find barriers between Us, the bystanders, and Them, our friends who are facing death. It is very important to recognize that these are society's barriers, not ones you have created on your own. Once you understand that you are struggling to overcome a block that society has put in your way, you've taken the first step toward being a truly helping friend to a dying patient, the first step toward knowing what to say.

I

TALKING AND LISTENING

1

Why Talk?
Why Listen?

If talking to someone who is terminally ill is so difficult, why try it? Why is it worth doing? What can you achieve by talking with and listening to someone who is seriously ill? One man, Steve, explained the enormous difference it made to his family. His wife, Susan, in her early thirties, developed leukemia. The shock was enormous — to her, to Steve, and to their three young children. But Susan found discussion impossible. She was deeply angry and upset, and as a result she could not talk normally to anyone about anything. Steve said that their house became wrapped in a tense and sullen silence. Although he had never done anything like it before, he arranged for the children to be looked after for a weekend, and booked Susan and himself into a motel. He said, "There was a lot of crying, some laughing and some drinking — each of which helped." After that weekend, Steve and Susan were able to talk normally, though, interestingly, they didn't spend a great deal of time afterward talking about the disease. In some respects the ghost that had blocked their communication had been exorcised.

In my experience, giving support and easing distress is a process that rewards both the donor and the recipient. These actions have worth and value because they strengthen your relationship. They create a new bond between you at a time when the strain of the illness might otherwise separate you. If you *don't* talk to each other you run a serious risk of ending up as strangers at a time when you most need to be friends, whereas if you do communicate, the reward is an enhanced relationship. There are several important points about dialogue which may seem obvious when you are calm and tranquil, but which are easily forgotten when you are under duress.

1. *Talking to Each Other Happens to Be the Best Method of Communication We Have*. There are, of course, many different ways of communicating — kissing, touching, laughing, frowning, even "not talking" (I'm reminded of the man who wanted to know why his wife hadn't spoken to him for three days, and his psychotherapist replied, "Perhaps she's trying to tell you something"). However, talking is our most efficient, most *specific* method of communication.

2. *Simply Talking about Distress Helps Relieve It*. There are many reasons for us to talk. There are obvious ones, such as telling children not to stick their fingers in the fan, telling a joke, asking about the results of a game or the horse race. But there are also less-obvious reasons for talking, among which is the simple desire to be listened to. In many circumstances, particularly when things go wrong,

people talk in order to get some trouble off their chest, and to be heard. You can see this quite often in the behavior of children. If you have an argument with your child, you may later hear him grumbling to his teddy bear, or even telling the bear off in the same way you scolded the child. Now this one-way talk is not exactly dialogue or conversation, but it serves a useful function. It releases a bit of pressure, and human beings can only stand so much pressure. There is relief to be found in talking. There is, therefore, a relief that *you* can provide for a sick person by listening and by simply *allowing* him to talk. You can help your friend even if you don't have all the answers.

In fact, "good listening" (which will be detailed in the next chapter) is known to be effective *in itself*. An interesting research study was done in the United States in which a number of totally untrained people were taught the simple techniques of good listening, and volunteer patients came to them to talk about their problems. The listeners in this study were not allowed to say or do anything at all. They just nodded and said "I see," or "Tell me more." They weren't allowed to ask questions of the patients or to say anything at all about the problems the patients described. At the end of the hour, almost all of the patients thought they had received very good therapy, and some of them telephoned the "therapists" to ask if they could see them again, and to thank them for the therapy. *You don't have to have the answers — just listening to the questions can help.*

3. *Thoughts That a Person Tries to Shut Out Will Do Harm Eventually.* One of the arguments friends and family put forward in order to *avoid* talking to the patient is

that talking about a fear or an anxiety might *create* an anxiety that didn't exist before the conversation. In other words, a friend might say to himself, "If I ask my friend whether he's worried about radiotherapy I might *make* him worried about it." Well, that doesn't happen. Studies done in Britain by psychologists talking to patients with terminal cancer suggest that conversations between patients and their relatives and friends do not create new fears and anxieties. In fact the opposite is true: *not* talking about a fear makes it bigger. Those patients with no one to talk to have a higher incidence of anxiety and depression. Several other researchers have shown that one of the biggest problems faced by terminally ill patients is that people won't talk to them, and the feelings of isolation add a great deal to their burden. When a major anxiety occupies a patient's mind, it is frequently very difficult for that patient to talk about anything at all.

Bottled-up feelings may also cause shame. Many people are ashamed of their fears and anxieties. They know that they are afraid of something, but they feel that they aren't "supposed" to be, and so feel ashamed. One of the greatest services you can do for your friend is to hear her fears and stay close once you've listened. By not backing away or withdrawing, you then show that you accept and understand her fears. This will help reduce the fear and the shame and help the patient regain her sense of perspective.

So for all these reasons you have everything to gain and nothing to lose by trying to talk and listen to someone who's seriously ill. It may seem awkward at the beginning, and it may seem that the patient doesn't want to talk. You may feel nervous and you may not want to talk either.

There are four types of obstacles to free communication between you and the patient. They are:

PATIENT	FRIEND OR RELATIVE
The patient wants to talk.	You don't.
The patient doesn't want to talk.	You do.
The patient wants to talk but feels he ought not to.	You don't know how to encourage him to talk.
The patient *appears* not to want to talk but really needs to.	You don't know what's best, and don't want to intervene if it makes things worse.

These may seem like major obstacles to communication, but you need not be alarmed. You can make yourself available for listening and talking without thrusting your offer down the patient's throat, and there are ways to work out whether the patient does or does not need to talk. It's all a question of "sensitive listening."

2

Sensitive Listening

Good listening is a very tricky art. Doctors are often as bad at it as anyone else. It is, however, relatively easy to turn yourself into a responsive and sensitive listener, by noting a few important details.

A lot depends on how you and your friend have spoken with each other in the past. However much you improve your ability to listen, you will not necessarily change your friend's usual style of communication. If your friend was always easy to talk to and if he spoke about his feelings freely, then he's likely to continue to do so. If, however, he has always been a private and closed person, it is not realistic to hope that you will convert him into "a good talker" just by becoming a good listener. Quite recently, I looked after two patients whose styles of communication within their marriages seemed initially similar. Joan and Peter, a couple in their late forties, seemed rather stiff and polite with each other. I wondered if they were not actually rather distant. However, during a time of medical crisis, I saw that in fact they were extremely close and were able to face some tough decisions about Joan's treatment by talking things through together. They told me that they had always talked about everything and shared all their concerns and fears, that they would carry on doing that now. They were, naturally, somewhat shy, but their normal way of communicating was well established and very useful. At first meeting Gillian and Bob seemed similar to Joan and Peter. However, as time went on, Gillian told me that she had always felt unsupported in times of crisis because Bob did not seem capable of facing the realities of the situation. He simply wasn't a good talker and listener, he felt uncomfortable talking about emotional issues, and he didn't really want Gillian to talk about them either. It was hard to raise important issues with them and they needed some help. While their basic patterns of talking didn't change, Bob gradually became less uncomfortable and was, as a result, of greater support to Gillian.

People do usually have their own preset styles of communication, some of which are adequate for the task of facing an illness, some of which, at first, are not. While sensitive listening may not alter the *fundamental* style, a great deal can still be achieved by working with whatever form of contact does exist.

By listening well you give the patient an *opportunity* to talk about the things she wants to talk about. That can make a big difference. Some people are hesitant to talk because they believe that their friends never really listen. In times of crisis, a good listener creates a radically different atmosphere. That may not always happen, however, so be careful not to set your expectations too high.

Good listening is both physical and mental. By knowing

the few simple rules that encourage free conversation, many of the most awkward gaps in communication can be avoided.

1. *Get the Setting Right.* The physical context of conversation is important enough to get the details correct at the start. Get comfortable, sit down, try to look relaxed (even if you don't feel it), try to signal the fact that you intend to spend some time with the patient (for instance, take your coat off!).

Keep your eyes on the same level as the person you're talking to. This almost always means sitting down. If, for instance, the patient is in a hospital bed and chairs are unavailable or too low, sitting on the bed is preferable to standing. All kinds of things can conspire against you in these circumstances; I've sometimes found on ward rounds that the only available chair is a commode. It may cause some minor embarrassment, but it's better than towering above someone as you try to talk sympathetically. In other circumstances, try to create as "private" an atmosphere as possible; don't try to talk in a corridor, or on a staircase. Conversations often go wrong because of these simple things. One patient, for example, herself a psychotherapist, didn't want to talk when I was sitting in her living room. But once I was in the hall with my coat on she felt less threatened and began to open up a bit. We both realized what was happening and, after we had talked in the hall for a while, I took my coat off and we went back into the living room. Despite the fact that we were both aware of what was going on, our behavior was almost involuntary! So, do try to create the right space, although however hard you try, interruptions — phones ringing, doorbells going, children coming in — are inevitable. You can only do your best to keep the atmosphere as warm, personal, and encouraging as possible.

Keep within a comfortable distance of the patient. Generally, there should be one to two feet of space between you. A longer distance makes dialogue feel awkward and formal, and a shorter distance can make the patient feel hemmed in, particularly if he is in bed and unable to back away. Try to make sure there are no physical obstacles (desks, bedside tables, and so on) between you. By simply offering that "it's not very easy to talk across this table, can I move it aside for a moment?" you can create a more comfortable atmosphere.

Keep looking at the person while you listen as well as while you talk. Eye contact tells the patient that the conversation is solely between the two of you. If, during a painful moment, you can't look directly into her eyes, at least stay close and hold the patient's hand, maintain contact in some way.

2. *Find Out Whether the Patient Wants to Talk.* It may be that the patient is simply not in the mood to talk, or even that he just does not want to talk to *you* that day. If that's the case, try not to be offended. If you're not sure what the patient wants, ask ("Do you feel like talking?") before you launch into a deep conversation ("Tell me about your feelings") when the patient may be tired or may have just finished talking to someone else.

3. *Listen and Show You're Listening.* When the patient is talking, you should try to listen to him, instead of thinking about what you're going to say next, and you should show that you're listening.

To listen properly, think carefully about what the patient is saying. Don't rehearse your reply, for doing so would mean that you're anticipating what you think the patient is *about* to say, rather than listening to what she *is* saying. Try not to interrupt the patient. If, on the other hand, she interrupts you, stop and let her say what she wants.

4. *Encourage the Patient to Talk.* Good listening is more than just sitting there like a running tape recorder. You can actually help the patient talk about what's on his mind by encouraging him. Simple things work very well. Try nodding, or offering affirmative comments like, "Yes," "I see," or "Tell me more." Those all sound simple, but at times of maximum stress it's the simple things that help things along.

You can also show that you're hearing — and listening — by repeating two or three words from the patient's last sentence. This technique does help the patient to feel that her words are being appreciated. Actually, when I teach medical students how to talk with patients I urge them to try this words-repetition technique with their friends. They invariably report that it moves the conversation along and makes the listener suddenly appear more interested and involved.

You can also reflect back to the talker what you've heard — partly to check that you've got it right, and partly to show that you're listening and trying to understand. Offer comments like, "So you mean that . . ." or, "If I've got that straight, you feel . . ." or even, "I hear you," although that last one might sound a bit self-conscious if it isn't your usual style.

5. *Don't Forget Silence and Nonverbal Communication.* If someone stops talking, it usually means that she is thinking about something painful or sensitive. Wait

with her for a moment — hold her hand or touch her — and then ask her what she was thinking about. Don't rush her, although silences at emotional moments often seem to last years.

Another point about silences is that sometimes you may think, "I don't know what to say" (hence the title of this book). On occasions, this may be because there isn't anything *to* say. So don't be afraid to say nothing and to just stay close. Sometimes a touch or an arm around the patient's shoulder is of greater value than anything you say.

Nonverbal communication can tell you much more about another person than you might have expected. I was recently caring for a middle-aged woman named Gladys, who seemed at first very angry and uncommunicative. I encouraged her to talk but she remained very "wrapped up." During one interview, while I was talking, I put my hand out to hers — rather tentatively, because I wasn't sure I was doing the right thing. To my surprise, she seized it, held it tightly, and wouldn't let go. The atmosphere changed instantly, and she started talking freely about her fears of further surgery and her fear of being abandoned by her family. The message with nonverbal contact is "Try it and see." If, for example, Gladys had not responded so positively, I would have been able to take my hand away and neither of us would have suffered any setback as a result of the effort.

6. *Don't Be Afraid to Describe Your Own Feelings.* You're allowed to say things like, "I find this difficult to talk about" or, "I'm not very good at talking about . . ." or even, "I don't know what to say." Describing your emotions is always valuable. I even encourage medical students to say such things when I teach them communication

skills. One of them came back to me after the course and said, "I tried what you told me — telling the patient that I found it awkward — and it *really worked*." Like the student, you may be pleasantly surprised.

7. *Make Sure You Haven't Misunderstood*. If you are sure you understand what the patient means, you can say so. Responses such as, "You sound very low" or, "That must have made you very angry" tell her that you've picked up the emotions she has been discussing or showing. But if you're not sure what the patient means, then ask: "What did that feel like?" "What do you think of it?" "How do you feel now?" Misunderstandings arise when you make assumptions. Peter, a family practitioner, was looking after a middle-aged woman with a terminal illness. The patient was a lawyer and had been in the hospital for several weeks before returning to her home weak and enfeebled. On one home visit she sighed and asked Peter, "How long will it be?" Peter was just about to tell her that she would probably die within the next few weeks, when he suddenly wondered whether she was really referring to her death. He hesitated and then asked her what she meant. She said, "I meant how long will it be before I can get back to work and be in court again." Relieved that he had not responded too quickly, Peter sat with her for a long time. They discussed how she thought she was doing, and he only answered her question after careful preparation.

Instinctively picking up what the patient is feeling is wonderful, but if you are slower to understand, don't hesitate to ask. Offering something like, "Help me understand what you mean" is quite useful.

8. *Don't Change the Subject.* If your friend wants to talk about how rotten he feels, let him. It may be difficult for you to listen to some of the things he is saying, but try to hear him out. If you find that you just can't handle the conversation at that moment, then suggest that you discuss it again later (you can even say this as simply as, "This is making me feel very uncomfortable at the moment, can we come back to it later?"). Don't change the subject before acknowledging the fact that your friend has raised it.

9. *Don't Give Advice Early.* Ideally, no one should give advice unless it's asked for. However, in this imperfect world we quite often find ourselves giving advice before we've been asked. Try not to give advice early in the conversation, because it stops dialogue. If you must advise, however, use helpful, modest phrases like: "Have you thought about trying . . ." or (if you're a born diplomat), "A friend of mine once tried . . ." Those are both less bald than, "If I were you I'd . . . ," which makes the patient think (or even say), "But you're not me" — a true conversation-stopper.

10. *Encourage Reminiscence.* Many patients — old and young — want to share reminiscences. Even children like to start stories about times when they were younger and want to hear you retell the events. For older patients reminiscences serve as reassurance that their lives have meaning. Sharing memories is often a bittersweet experience for them and for you. It may remind them of how much they're losing by dying. It may make you both cry. In practice, many psychotherapists and counselors use reminiscence (the so-called guided autobiography) to encourage a patient to positively look at her past. Barbara, a

patient in her late seventies, was having a very tough time talking to her sons about the way she felt about the present situation. I asked her about her past and what it was like when her children were young. It so happened that this was actually a very good time for the family. She brightened as she talked about her sons, and for the first time her emotions seemed fresh and vivid. So I encouraged her to start talking to her sons about that time, and the air seemed to clear between them. They were reminded of their past closeness, and that helped them to feel closer in the current situation.

Another thing that may emerge from recovered memories is the way the patient has coped with previous setbacks — the loss of a job, a marital problem, a car accident. Patients may think that they "simply can't cope," but when they go back over the past they find that they have the personality to handle all kinds of problems quite well. Sometimes, as a result of thinking about the past, the patient realizes that she can draw on her past coping abilities now.

11. *Respond to Humor.* Many people imagine that there cannot possibly be anything to laugh about if you are seriously ill or dying. They are missing an extremely important point about humor. Humor actually serves an important function in our way of coping with major threats and fears: it allows us to *ventilate,* to rid ourselves of intense feelings while putting things in perspective. Humor is one of the ways human beings deal with things that seem at first impossible to deal with.

If you think for a moment about the most common subjects of jokes, you'll realize they include mothers-in-law, fear of flying, hospitals, doctors, and sex. None of those subjects is intrinsically funny. An argument with a mother-in-law, for instance, can be distressing for all concerned, but arguing with the mother-in-law has been an easy laugh for the stand-up comedian for centuries, because we all laugh most easily at the things with which we cope least easily. We laugh at things to put them in perspective, to reduce them in size and threat.

One patient I particularly remember was a woman in her early forties. She had cancer of the cervix which eventually necessitated an in-dwelling catheter in her bladder. While she was in the hospital she carried her drainage bag like a purse, loudly suggesting that it was a shame nobody made a drainage bag that matched her gloves. Out of context that may sound ghoulish, or like "gallows humor," but for this particular woman that humor helped her with a very distressing problem. It demonstrated, I think, her true bravery and her desire to rise above physical problems. Maintaining, and using, her sense of humor was very much in character.

From this experience and many others that I have shared with patients, I have become convinced that laughter helps the patient to get a handle on his situation. If he wants to use humor, even humor that to an outsider might seem black humor, you should certainly encourage him. It clearly helps him cope. But don't try to cheer him up with a supply of your own jokes. You can best help your friend by responding sensitively to his humor, rather than by trying to set the mood with your own.

I have one further comment about the subject of humor and illness. A number of people subscribe to the belief that laughter actually cures some physical illnesses. I remain very skeptical about this. While there's no doubt that laughter makes you feel better, raising your pain threshold and possibly reducing the intensity of symptoms, among other benefits, I would need more convincing before I would believe that it significantly affects disease processes.

In summary, the objective of sensitive listening is to understand as completely as you can what the other person is feeling. You can never achieve complete understanding, but the closer you get, the better the communication between you and your friend will be. *The more you try to understand your friend's feelings, the more support you are giving.*

3

Why You
Need to Know
What's Going On

Nothing in this book can, unfortunately, alter what is happening to your friend. But understanding his illness can change its impact on you and the relationship between you.

By comprehending what is happening and having some guidelines in your mind, you can change the way you respond. This happens in three ways:

1. *By Your Own Understanding and Recognition of What Your Friend Is Going Through.* This will reduce your own fear and pain, allowing you to function more normally in very abnormal circumstances.

2. *By Reacting Differently Yourself.* Once you identify the different emotions and feelings that your friend is experiencing, you can respond differently. For instance, you may be able to turn a potential argument into something that helps you both and brings you closer.

3. *By Having Some Guidelines with Which to Work*. Guidelines will stop you from feeling overwhelmed. The husband of a patient of mine told me how he felt when he and his wife first realized that her breast cancer had recurred in her spinal column. "I felt absolutely paralyzed. I had no idea what to do at all. I felt as if I just wanted to curl up in a ball and wish it all away. There were a hundred thoughts and a thousand questions going through my mind and I had absolutely no idea what to try and do first. So I felt as if I couldn't do anything, that I'd never come out of that tailspin."

By better understanding what happens to someone who becomes more ill and faces the threat of death, you will be able to reduce that sensation of paralysis. You will be better able to plan, and you will continue to be resourceful.

In these three ways you can prepare yourself for some of the things that will happen. A simple example shows how understanding the nature of an emotion can change your behavior. Let us pick anger as a fairly common reaction with which everybody is familiar. We all have arguments among our family and friends and we all react quite naturally if someone is angry with us: we either apologize, get angry back, or ignore it. These are the normal ways of reacting to somebody who's angry with us.

When, however, somebody in your family or circle is facing a serious illness and death, the anger that she feels might really be directed at the illness; it comes out directed at you because you are the only person around. If you are aware of the fact that the anger isn't *meant* for you personally, then you might be able to respond in a way different from the typical family-argument style. You might help the patient defuse her anger and talk about it constructively instead of simply boiling with it. Here's an example of what I mean:

The patient says:
"I feel dreadful and you're no help."

↓

You have several choices:

| If you react "normally" (as in a family argument) you might say: | But if you realize that the anger is not directed at you personally, you might say: |

If you react "normally" (as in a family argument) you might say:

↓

"Well, I'm doing my best."

or

"Stop criticizing me."

or

"You're not easy to help."

↓

All of these responses lead to escalation and a rift between you.

But if you realize that the anger is not directed at you personally, you might say:

↓

"How dreadful do you feel?"

or

"What's the most dreadful part?"

or

"You sound really low."

↓

All of these responses encourage a dialogue and allow the patient to say more about what's on his mind.

One example of this working was given to me by Brian, whose wife, Pat, was a patient of mine. The stress and pressure of their careers and family life had increased considerably during Pat's illness. I tried showing them communication patterns similar to the diagram above. A few days later, Brian said to me, "You know, we always used to have arguments that began with Pat saying, 'You never remember to take the garbage out on Wednesdays,' or 'You always leave the garden gate unlatched,' or something, and I would usually reply with, 'Oh yeah? Well *you* never remember to turn the thermostat down when you go out,' or something like that. And it would build up. Well, when she was in the hospital, and I brought her the wrong magazine, she said, 'You never remember the magazine I like best,' and instead of arguing I suddenly thought about what it was like for her. I said how I thought it must be awful lying in the hospital not being able to get things for herself and how much she must have been looking forward to seeing her favorite magazine, and suddenly we weren't having an argument at all, but suddenly felt very close. It was a great surprise to both of us, I think."

I will give several similar examples of sensitive responses in the rest of this book. If you are able to understand something of *why* the patient is saying what she is saying, then you may be able to respond in a way that eases her pain. That way, you become part of the solution; if you *don't* realize what's going on, there's a danger you may become part of the problem.

II
THE PROCESS
OF DYING

4

The Transition

Very few healthy people actually *want* to die, and very few seriously ill patients hasten their own death. We are all "programmed" to hold on to life for as long as possible. This means that if somebody tells us we have an illness that may kill us, we may find accepting that prognosis as fact difficult. Everybody facing the threat of death has to make a painful transition from thinking of himself as a perfectly healthy person to thinking of himself as somebody who might die, and then as somebody who *will* die. One can think of this transition as going from "It won't happen to me (although I know one day it might)," to "It really might happen to me," to "It's happening to me."

The transition consists of many stages, and it's difficult — no matter what age you are and what the nature of the illness is. In fact, I well remember two patients, both suffering from advanced breast cancer, who happened to be in adjacent rooms in a hospital.

Connie was in her mid-thirties and was very near the end of her life when I first met her. She and her husband had talked over every aspect of her dying, and had made all the arrangements for her to die at their home. She spoke sadly but lovingly of the beautiful view from her front room. She asked me to make sure that she was released from the hospital as soon as possible, so that she could spend her last few days looking at that view. She was an incredibly impressive woman. Her courage and calm struck a chord with everybody around her. She got her wish. In the next room was a woman called Barbara who was in her early seventies. Barbara was no less likable, but she was simply not ready to die. She had great difficulty adjusting to her physical handicaps and had even greater difficulty trying to sort out her family (she had two sons and a stepson who were bickering and arguing with each other). Barbara was very distressed by what was going on, and needed a lot of time and support. Only after several interviews did she begin to adjust her view of what was happening. Then she was able to make the many plans and arrangements that made things easier for her and for her family.

The point is that for everyone going through this transition, no matter how old or young, there is a huge task of adjustment, and this is a time when a close friend and relative can be of real help.

To make it easier to understand what goes on during this transition, I have divided it into three phases: a beginning phase as the person faces the threat of death; an illness phase as the person's pattern of living becomes altered by physical decline; and a final phase as the person approaches death. Of course, any such division is intrinsically artificial, but in my experience as a doctor (and relative) I have found these three phases easy to understand and useful as a way of getting a handle on a continuous, and possibly confusing process. In some respects, the process is similar to a trip or a journey; it may be difficult to pinpoint when "traveling" turns into "nearly there," but nevertheless there are easily identifiable differences in the atmosphere between mid-journey and "nearly there." I am not claiming that there is anything unique in this division; it is simply a practical description.

The pioneer of thinking in this area is Dr. Elisabeth Kübler-Ross. I mention her work because many readers may know about it and wonder if I am striking out on my own or trying to disprove her views. In fact, I differ only in some minor respects.

Dr. Kübler-Ross divided the process of dying into five stages: denial, anger, bargaining, depression, and acceptance. While she highlighted five extremely important aspects of dying, in my view she described types of *reactions* rather than phases. I find that there are many kinds of reactions other than those five, including fear, anxiety, hope, and guilt. Some kinds of reactions are common near the beginning, some are more common during the illness, and some are more common at the end. Many people, for example, are angry and depressed at the beginning but become more accepting near the end. So, rather than follow the Kübler-Ross scheme, I am going to discuss the most common kinds of reaction in each of the three phases I've mentioned. There is no right and wrong about this. We are all simply looking for easily understood, useful ways of describing this important transition. I hope that my description makes the process intelligible and gives you some guidelines to helping your friend through the various phases.

However, before going on to the details of these reactions, there are a few general points that need underlining. First of all, each one of us is capable of feeling several emotions at the same time (this may sound obvious but it's easy to forget). Think what happens when a child gets separated from a parent in a shop or a crowd. When they find each other the parent is usually immensely relieved and pleased, but also angry with the child for getting lost. She may also feel a tinge of guilt for having lost her concentration for a moment. Now if I were describing such a scene to you, I would mention the relief, the anger, and the guilt separately — even though they crop up simultaneously. And that's what I'm doing in this book. I know I'm describing a mixture of emotions, but I can only do it one ingredient at a time. It's important not to forget that *all human beings are capable of experiencing several different emotions at the same time.*

Second, even though I'm going to describe the transition in three phases, these aren't hard-and-fast rules followed by every patient. People facing death often go forward and backward in their understanding of what's going on. A patient may reach acceptance of his situation on Monday, then show denial or anger on Tuesday. It's no help for the friend to get annoyed and say something like, "Hey, wait a minute, you understood it all yesterday, you're not supposed to be angry again today." Nor does that sort of change mean that you, as the friend, have misunderstood the situation. You have to be aware that human emotions change constantly, like waves and eddies on a beach within the easily recognizable major change of the tide coming in. Even the conceptually neatest considerations of this process have their limitations. No one goes through the process of dying in regimented textbook fashion.

It's particularly important that you understand the lack of order and predictability, precisely because the patterns are so variable and individual. Some people are already physically very ill at the time of first diagnosis. They may even be near death. Others may feel physically fit at the time of diagnosis, and may, as a result, have great difficulty in believing that they have a lethal condition. Similarly, some people will adjust to the ending of their life relatively early in the course of the disease while others will never allow themselves to accept the imminence of death. As long as you are aware of this wide variation, then you won't be put off by it, and will be able to offer steady support to your friend as he experiences different emotions.

The last general point I want to make is this: in most illnesses there is a measure of uncertainty — and sometimes there seems to be nothing but uncertainty. Will the pain be relieved? How long will the patient live? Is there any hope at all? To many of these vital questions, there may be no answer. It may not be possible for doctors (or anyone else) to tell how long the patient may live or what the future will be like. Most people find that living with that kind of uncertainty is awful. In my own case, my illness began with several unusual and intermittent problems and diagnosis was not clear for many months. It was very difficult to cope with the thought that "something is wrong but nobody knows what it is." I also came under considerable pressure from friends and family who thought that I should be rushing around the world seeing international experts to get The Answer. This was a difficult time because none of us knew how or for what to prepare ourselves. When the diagnosis later became clear, and I learned, as I put it, "the name of the beast," it became easier to face facts and to make appropriate plans. In retrospect, that time of uncertainty was a major strain. As many psychotherapists have often said — and it cannot be overstressed — *"Living with uncertainty is painful in itself."*

5

Facing the Threat

🐎 Whether your friend is feeling physically well or extremely ill when the diagnosis is made, there is still the moment at which he comes up against the threat of the end of life, not as an idea or as something that happens to other people, but as a probability or certainty. This requires vast mental adjustments. Freda, for instance, was a young woman whose once-treated cancer of the ovary recurred. She had always been a rather introverted woman, inclined to be highly anxious (which was neither surprising nor abnormal), and very dependent on her husband. When I told them both that the tumor had recurred, she did some unusual things. She began to moan — almost to wail — and she started pacing up and down the consultation room faster and faster, speaking in disjointed fragments and repeating phrases over and over again. Her husband was appalled and kept saying, "Freda, why are you behaving like this? This *isn't you*." But actually it *was* she; this was her way of reacting to extreme and abnormal circumstances. In the face of that very great abnormality, her behavior was, for her, normal. As the friend and supporter of a patient, you will need to widen your own view of what might be regarded as normal in very abnormal circumstances.

Behavior is quite varied under these circumstances, simply because human minds are not very good at coping with bad news in the abstract. When we hear news that may drastically affect our future, we find it difficult to get a fix on it. Several different kinds of reactions may emerge from our struggle to come to terms with the news. Some of these reactions may seem somewhat bizarre. But if you try to understand the conditions under which they arise you will find them easier to deal with.

Even if you're currently caring for someone who was given his diagnosis some time ago, even years ago, I hope you'll continue reading this section. Reactions that begin at the time of diagnosis continue throughout the whole illness, and those reactions may, even in retrospect, shed some light on the patient's current state of mind.

THE PATIENT'S FEELINGS

Shock and Disbelief

Most of us often use words like "shock" and "disbelief" to describe trivial things. We are simply indicating that events are a little unusual: "It always rains the day I get the windows cleaned — I don't believe it." When an event is beyond the range of day-to-day living to the point that the patient may have serious difficulty comprehending it, it's often quite difficult for her to find the right words to express her feelings. Almost every patient facing the threat of terminal illness and death goes through a phase of shock and disbelief, whether measured in hours or days, or whether so prolonged that she never seems to emerge from it completely.

True disbelief prevents the patient from incorporating the diagnosis into his view of the world. The disbelieving patient may be able to think normally, in spurts. The patient may be able to appreciate the news one evening yet wake up the next morning wondering whether it is real after all. Elizabeth, a patient of mine with cancer of the colon, quite often said, "I keep on thinking it's all a dream." This sort of genuine disbelief is a completely normal reaction to overwhelming news.

Shock, on the other hand, suggests a fuller impact on the patient's ability to think and behave. While Elizabeth, although feeling as if she were in a dream, functioned quite normally at home and at work, another patient, Jennifer, temporarily lost her decision-making abilities. She was unable to carry on her work in a public relations firm, and was upset to find that she couldn't even make the simple decision of ordering a meal in a restaurant. A patient in shock finds it difficult to experience normal thoughts and emotions. Shock, like disbelief, waxes and wanes. The most common symptom is a breakdown in the ability to make decisions, as with Jennifer. In a state of shock even relatively simple decisions seem impossible. Other symptoms include forgetfulness — the patient may not remember familiar phone numbers and names. A patient in shock may also slow down. Simple actions, like getting dressed or cooking meals, may take a very long time. The patient may go shopping, for instance, and forget why she's there. She may often seem to be staring into space or to be lost to the outside world for a time. Often, the person in this state seems to be inert and apathetic. But there is a caldron of emotions mixing and bubbling inside her. The patient may also cling and accept a loss of independence in her desire to be cared for in what may (at first) seem a very child-like way.

Shock is, then, a highly unpleasant and distressing state. Often it is made worse because the patient realizes that he is in trouble, and feels that he should be able to simply snap out of it. No one simply snaps out of shock. This normal (but severe) reaction to overwhelming news is, however, a phase. Most people do not recover instantly, or by simply "pulling themselves together," but instead recover gradually over time.

As time goes on, then, the sensation should fade. If, however, the state of shock extends and the patient shows no signs of regaining normal functions, you may need to get some expert help. It is worth discussing this with the patient's doctor.

Denial

There is a real difference between "denial" and "disbe-lief." Disbelief can be summarized as "I *can not* take this in (even though I'm trying)." Denial is "I *will not* take this on board (even though I could)." Denial can happen at several levels. It can be completely involuntary or it can be partly voluntary. Sometimes the patient might *appear* to be trying to come to terms with the situation even as he has subcon-sciously "decided" to block it off.

Denial does not indicate that the patient is unintelligent or losing his mind. A very well-known physician was ad-mitted to his own hospital for an exploratory operation. It showed that he had advanced cancer of the pancreas which was, in his case, incurable. He was told the diagnosis a few days after the operation by the surgeon, but every day after that he asked the surgeon the same question, "What did the operation show?" The surgeon, who knew the patient well as a colleague and as a friend, answered each day, "It showed cancer of the pancreas — we told you yesterday." To which the patient would always answer, "Oh yes, of course — you told me yesterday." He would then ask the same question the following day. It was nearly two weeks before the patient found that he could truly remember the diagnosis.

Another doctor, a family practitioner who developed cancer of the prostate, told me that after the diagnosis was made, "It wasn't as if I couldn't believe the diagnosis, I was just absolutely *certain* in my heart that it wasn't cancer. I assumed there was a mix-up with the laboratory result. Actually I didn't just *think* there was a mistake — I was absolutely *sure* of it. I even telephoned the pathologist. When he told me it was cancer of the prostate, I just thought he'd made the same mistake as everyone else. I knew all about the process of denial in other people — I'd seen it many times with my patients when I had to tell them bad news. But while all this was going on with me, I was sure that this wasn't a case of denial at work. I just kept on feeling, 'This isn't prostate cancer, it isn't happening to me — it's not my turn yet.' The feelings only began to fade after three weeks, nearly a month."

The important point is that denial is a conflict between knowledge and belief. While the patient's mind is telling him that what is happening *is* real, the emotion of denial can be so powerful that the person is simply unable to believe the facts.

As someone close to the patient, you should be aware of the power of denial. If you underestimate that power,

you might think your friend is being silly or even losing
his mind. But denial is a normal coping mechanism of
the human mind. In time it will usually fade away, allowing the patient to accept the bad news without being
swamped.

Another reason for being aware of the power of denial is
that you cannot wipe it out by simply *confronting* the
patient with the facts. Although that approach might seem
sensible ("I'll just tell him what's really going on"), in
practice it does not achieve anything. You put yourself
in the position of an adversary to the patient. As I shall illustrate later, there are ways in which you can leave the
door open for discussion without actually challenging
the patient.

Sometimes, then, denial can be a powerful and involuntary reaction to threatening news. On other occasions, it
can be quite plain and direct. Several patients have given
me fairly clear guidelines about what they will or will not
listen to. Several times, I've been told, "Don't tell me any
bad news, Doctor — if it's serious talk to my wife."

In those circumstances, the patient may know deep
down how bad the news is, but may not, at the moment,
want to face it in the open. This may be a perfectly useful
way for the person to cope with the news, either temporarily or even permanently, if there is no pressing need for him
to know precisely what's going on. But this raises a most
important issue: Does the patient *need* to know what's
going on? In other words, does denial matter? Is it necessary for the patient to face up to the bald facts? This is a
most important question when it comes to facing bad
news, and it's worth looking at from several different
viewpoints.

Some doctors specializing in the care of the dying suggest that facing the news is absolutely essential, that you simply cannot approach the end of your life properly unless you face death directly and learn to accept it. On the other hand, many families of patients feel differently. They think that the knowledge itself will hasten the end of her life and rob her of her will to live. ("Don't tell our mother she's got cancer," they may ask. "The news alone would kill her.")

Keeping patients uninformed is not helpful from the medical point of view. Several studies of patients in cancer wards show that the majority of patients really do want to know exactly what's going on, and that they *need* to know in order to make intelligent plans. Furthermore, studies comparing the mental state of patients kept unaware with those who do know show that patients who are kept in the dark have far greater problems with depression, anxiety, and a sense of isolation.

In my own practice I have listened to many patients describe these feelings of isolation, mistrust, and (sometimes) desperation. Most of these feelings faded away when the patient was given the information he wanted.

One patient was an intelligent businessman in his early thirties who for six years had experienced occasional unsteadiness in his walking and pins and needles around his face. He had, in fact, early (and fairly mild) multiple sclerosis, but two successive doctors refused to tell him what was wrong. He said not being told what was wrong was just like going to his bank, asking for the balance of his account, and being told that "it isn't anything to worry about," and that he should "go home and not think about it." When he was told the diagnosis by a third doctor, he felt a sense of relief at finally being treated as a human being and an equal. He felt that his previous doctors had insulted him and patronized him by withholding vital information.

If we feel angry and insulted when something as simple as our bank balance is withheld from us, we are likely to feel much more insulted when something of far greater significance, such as the state of our health and future, is withheld. Most people do want to know. Several studies by physicians of patients with newly diagnosed cancers have shown that at least 50 percent, and perhaps as many as 80 percent, of patients would like to know what's going on. The medical profession is slowly accepting this information. Nowadays the kind of doctor who never tells the patient the facts is something of a rarity.

If a patient wants to know what is going on, he must be told. To do anything else is unfair and unjust. Not only that, but withholding information may be infringing on the patient's ethical, moral, and (in some countries) legal rights. Prompted by legal precedence, particularly in the United States, the medical profession is coming to accept that a patient has a *right* to information that concerns him, and that the decision as to whether to exercise that right or not is the patient's alone.

What If the Patient Doesn't Want to Know?

If it appears that the patient does not want to know, there are two criteria by which you can assess the situation: is there any particular *need* for the patient to know; is the patient becoming *distressed* by not knowing?

There may be several needs that cannot be addressed unless the patient is fully in the picture. Medical needs, such as treatment choices and options, often cannot be offered unless the patient understands the nature and gravity of the disease. This is often the case with AIDS and cancer treatments, which usually cannot be given unless the patient is aware of the need for them and of their side effects. I have a very vivid memory of Ellen, a patient with cancer of the ovary. She was a senior personnel officer in a large corporation, but her doctor told me, "She will simply not allow me to tell her what is going on, and I am concerned that you may not be able to offer her treatment." She was an exceptionally nervous woman and her first words to me were, "If it's cancer, I don't want you to tell me." I assured her that I would not and asked about her fears of cancer. She told me of the previous deaths of five members of her family and of the sufferings that they had endured. She feared suffering in a similar manner, and thought that if she *knew* it was cancer, all the fight would go out of her. Without specifying the name of her disease, I described the treatment, its side effects, and the various support services that we could offer (including more conversations to help allay her fears). She recognized the treatment as chemotherapy. When I confirmed that it was, she smiled broadly (for the first time) and said, "Oh, well, I knew it was cancer anyway." From that moment on, she relaxed and tolerated the treatments and the ups and downs of her disease with considerable calm.

The medical needs of a patient may dictate the sharing of the diagnosis. Patients who may appear not to want to know may know very well what is going on, but they need a supportive atmosphere to share their fears. As the patient's friend, you do not have to force a confrontation to deal with the apparent denial. While this type of situation is of greater importance in the relationship between the patient and doctor, you as friend and supporter should know that the patient must, occasionally, be fully informed for medical reasons.

There may be other reasons for a patient to know what is going on. These may include plans for business, for buying or selling homes, for arranging trips and holidays, or for any number of family and personal reasons. Most of us make decisions about things like this all the time, assuming that we are going to live at least long enough to see the completion of the plans. Confronted with a serious illness, we might well make different plans. Supporters and friends of the patient should think about whether the patient is making plans that would be altered by the news. Is he saving up for a cruise? Has he made long-term investments, such as saving for his young son's college education? Is he just about to enter a big business venture that may be jeopardized by physical incapacity? If so, you will need to further explore the sharing of the news (and I shall be explaining more about how to do this later).

Let us suppose, however, that the patient has no medical reasons and no important family reasons to know about the future. What then? Is denial acceptable in these circumstances? Or should the facts be thrust upon the patient until they are fully understood? The single most important consideration is the distress of the patient. If the patient is completely calm and tranquil, and communicates freely and functions normally *without* knowing what's going on, then friends, family, and doctors should not thrust the facts at the patient.

If, on the other hand, the patient is apparently saying, "I don't want to know, don't tell me," but is, in the process, suffering from much distress, the situation can often be improved by sharing the facts. Quite often the patient really *wants* to ask the questions but feels that she is not *brave* enough to cope with the answers. This is an exceptionally difficult situation to handle, and you should seek assistance from sympathetic and skilled helpers (whether they are doctors, nurses, social workers, clergy, or psychologists) if you find yourself supporting a patient in this state.

Annie, for instance, was twenty-three years old and dying of a rare cancer that had proved resistant to all forms of therapy. When I first met her she was paralyzed from the mid-chest region downward, had difficulty breathing (because of secondary tumors in her lungs), and was in moderate to severe pain as a result of other tumors pressing on several nerves. Bright and intelligent, she had obviously been (before the changes due to the illness and the treatment) an attractive woman. At first meeting, it seemed to me that she was absolutely determined not to acknowledge how serious her condition was. Her sister (herself a doctor) told me that Annie was in great pain at home and needed high doses of painkillers, but put on a brave front for her visits to the hospital (including taking a great deal of trouble over her makeup). I wanted to improve control of the pain, but Annie simply said that everything was fine and that she only experienced minor pain now and then. She also denied that she was short of breath, even though she labored to finish a whole sentence.

She was absolutely determined to hold back any indication that things weren't going well. Her mother and father, with whom she was very close, were deeply distressed both by Annie's physical condition and by the way she wouldn't let anybody "in" to help her.

It was clear to me that Annie did not want to be seen as someone who had failed the medical team that had done its best for her. Near the end of our second conversation, she mentioned a dream that she'd had about a friend of hers, Jenny, who had tragically committed suicide a few years previously. In the dream Annie and Jenny were riding together on a bus. Jenny would not allow Annie to get off, telling her that she was staying on the bus to the end of the journey. This was the only indication Annie had shown me that she even thought about dying, and I asked her if she would see our clinic chaplain, John Martin.

John's two interviews with Annie accomplished a very great deal in a relatively short time. Annie revealed that Jenny had not said anything to Annie to indicate that she was contemplating suicide. Annie told John about the rage that she felt at Jenny's death. "If only she'd told me what she was feeling," said Annie, "we could have talked about so much." John replied, "Does that sound familiar?" Suddenly Annie realized how much *she* was holding back from her family, and how angry and distressed she made *them* feel, just as Jenny had left her angry and distressed. For the first time in the hospital, Annie cried. She explained that she was trying to protect her family from what was happening by not talking to them. John showed her that she was in fact excluding her family and hurting them. But he made sure that she knew that the feelings she was experiencing were normal rather than any shameful sign of weakness.

At the end of the interview Annie acknowledged openly her fear and pain. She admitted that perhaps it wasn't such a good idea to work so hard at maintaining a front and hiding her feelings. "Thank you," she told John, "for giving me the courage not to be courageous." We later heard that in the next few days she was able to tell her parents how much she loved them and that she wanted to be able to say good-bye to them but found it difficult. She was also able to communicate more freely with her sister. Annie died a few weeks later.

Denial can be damaging to both family and patient. As friend and caregiver, you may need to call in some expert and willing help if the immediate helpers are being excluded, as Annie's family and I were. It may well be that the chaplain or minister is in the best position, but if your friend doesn't have strong religious convictions, other helpers such as social workers, psychologists, or nurses may be able to achieve this. This kind of denial is hard on the patient, on you, and on anyone who has to look after the patient.

In summary, information should always be offered, but sometimes it is rejected. If there is no medical or social need to deal with that information, then you, as the friend of the patient, can be comfortable in leaving the denial alone, and in accepting it as the way in which this particular patient is dealing with the threat. If, on the other hand, there are reasons that the patient *must* know what's going on, or if the denial is causing the patient great distress, you should look for some expert help to allow the patient to decide whether to continue denial or to face the facts.

Anger

Anger is common in any illness, but with simple and self-limiting illnesses — flu, for example — the anger fades as the patient recovers. With chronic illness, the anger is there every day.

Perhaps the angriest patient I ever met was Helena. She was thirty-two when cancer of the cervix was diagnosed. A homosexual who had been in a stable relationship with her partner Andrea for many years, Helena was enraged by her disease. She hated the symptoms and the pain, she hated the way it interfered with her sexuality and her lifestyle, she hated being "in the power" of doctors and hospitals, and since her disease originated from a virus caught during her heterosexual contacts in her teens, she hated men (including me). While it was difficult to listen as she articulated these various aspects of her rage, it seemed to me that each aspect of her anger was in some ways justifiable, and certainly understandable. I think most people, facing disruption of everything they loved, would feel exactly the same way.

So why do we get angry when we're ill? The single most important reason, as in Helena's case, is loss of control. Most of us try hard to establish control over our lives, at all stages and at all times. We make, and expect always to be able to make, personal choices and decisions. Generally speaking we don't like it when we have no say in events. Much of the rage and unhappiness that is caused when a factory is closed down, for instance, is due to the feelings of powerlessness experienced by the people thrown out of work. Of course not everyone is like this. Some fatalists genuinely enjoy living with decisions and choices made by other people, or made at random; but by and large, most of us would prefer that things happened our way.

The problem is that illness *doesn't* happen our way. It happens its own way. And in exactly the same way a factory worker resents the powerlessness forced on him by a closure, so someone who is ill often resents the loss of control over his own body and his own fate.

Patients experience three major types of anger:

a. Anger at the rest of the world, including friends, relatives, and all other survivors of the patient. (You could call this the "why me?" anger.)

b. Anger directed at any recognizable form of fate or destiny or controlling influence that has allowed this to happen (for people with religious beliefs this anger may be directed at God, or may cause a loss of religious faith).

c. Anger at anyone trying to help, particularly doctors and nurses (the "blaming the bearer for the bad news" reaction).

Anger at everyone who is healthy is an extremely common emotion. "Why me?" crops up so often in television plays and films that the question may seem to be nothing more than a cliché. In reality, it is a genuine and deeply felt emotion. Although "why me?" can sometimes sound like a question, it is generally a cry of anger, often worsened by frustration and desperation. Ted, who had a rare lymphoma, directed his anger straight at me. "Why should I get this illness?" he asked. "I've been healthy all my life and I've watched my diet and I've exercised every day. You don't do that, do you? I've seen you buying junk food from the vending machines for lunch and eating potato chips and chocolate instead of proper food [which was true] — why should I have this disease and not you?" There is no one simple answer to that kind of anger. Many illnesses have no relationship to the previous health of the person. These illnesses are nothing more than the product of mischance and bad luck. I explained this to Ted, and told him directly that his lymphoma and my relative health had nothing to do with the value or quality of either of us as people. Remember that for a great many medical conditions, the difference between the patient and anybody else is luck, and nothing else.

As a friend of the patient, then, you might easily be the target of that anger. While it may not seem fair that you should be the first in the firing line, it does happen quite often. This anger is certainly not abnormal, nor should it be construed as a sign of something fundamentally wrong in the relationship between you and the patient.

Remember that you should respond to "why me?" as you would to a cry of pain or despair, rather than by trying to *answer* it as a question. I shall illustrate various ways of responding to "why me?" at the end of this chapter.

The second kind of anger — directed against fate or God — is also common and very real. We shall be dealing with that in greater detail when we discuss spiritual aspects. This kind of anger raises very fundamental questions about the way the patient sees the whole world. It is not the kind of reaction that can be passed off with a consoling phrase.

The third kind of common, if complex, anger is specifically directed at the people who are trying to help. This anger can be extraordinarily strong — as I discovered during one of my own spells of hospitalization. I was trying to write a medical research paper (typical of my own denial combined with guilt that I wasn't achieving anything while I was ill). I asked my wife to bring a large bag of case records to the hospital so that I could work on them. She arrived over an hour late. I was totally consumed by rage. At the time my anger seemed logical. I was stuck in the hospital, trying (pseudoheroically) to make a contribution to medicine, and where was she? In fact, of course, she was pushed to the limit by the combination of her own job, the family, the household, and my illness. My rage had everything to do with the illness and nothing to do with her. However, she was the only person around, and she got all my abuse. It's something I'm still ashamed of, even though I now understand how it happened.

So anger can be projected — painfully, personally, and directly — at you, the friend and supporter. It can also be directed at other helpers, particularly doctors and nurses, and this may later rebound in several ways, making it even more difficult for you to help the patient. You may, for instance, be asked to take sides and judge between patient and doctor. Or, because of your involvement with the patient, you may find yourself pitted against the doctor. While I am not, of course, implying that doctors never deserve to be blamed, on many occasions the blame is really directed against the disease, not the doctor.

The transaction between doctor and patient superficially resembles many other normal transactions of daily life. Society (and the medical profession) have endowed a consultation with a doctor with the same sort of expectations as, say, a consultation with a garage mechanic. Many patients hope (and perhaps expect) that the doctor will repair the illness in their body in the same way that a mechanic repairs a dent in a car. But in a doctor's office, unlike a garage, there are no guarantees. If the disease turns out to be incurable, the tendency will be for the patient to be angry because his expectations have not been met. The more modern medicine comes to resemble a business, the more patients expect the rights of a paying customer, and the more difficult it becomes to realize that many diseases are simply not fixable.

This fact underscores the reasons why patients become angry when they are dealing with a disease and why they commonly (at some stage in the illness) blame the doctor for the illness. You may become involved in this kind of a reaction as a bystander called in to adjudicate, or you may become the target of the anger yourself. This is a common form of reaction to serious illness, and although the vehement anger directed at you may seem highly personal, it isn't really personal at all.

Fear

Fear of serious illness and death is common, expected, and accepted by society. But if fear of dying was something with which we all could cope, this book would be unnecessary. Our fear of dying is, however, complex in nature, and demands particular attention.

One of the most common fears is the *fear of being afraid*. Most of us have an idea at the back of our minds that we're not *supposed* to be afraid of things. Of course, almost everybody is afraid of something. Even people who strenuously deny that they're afraid of anything may be afraid — perhaps, for instance, they are afraid of admitting that they have one or two fears. Arlene was a fifty-one-year-old woman with breast cancer. Her speech was slow and vague, and I found myself getting very irritated each time we met. At one stage I suggested she bring some member of her family along to help communication, and she asked her son and daughter-in-law to contact me. At a separate interview they told me that Arlene was utterly terrified of what was going on. Far from being stupid or dull-witted, she had correctly estimated her medical situation and was equally scared by treatment and by what might happen if she opted against treatment. She was literally almost speechless with fright. Armed with a new understanding of her particular fear I went back to Arlene and started all over again. The difference was amazing — once she realized that she didn't have to be ashamed or frightened of the fear itself, she was able to articulate her fears in detail, with a command and understanding of her situation which impressed and surprised both of us.

In looking closely at the fears that can have these profound effects, two important points must be considered. First, fear requires an imagination. A person with no imagination whatsoever could not imagine any of the possible consequences of what's going on and could not be frightened. People who are afraid are *thinking* and are *imagining*. It is one disadvantage of having an active and functioning mind. Whatever else you may think, fear is not a sign of stupidity or "low moral fiber."

Second, fear of dying is not one fear but many fears. Every person has a different list of fears about death. You might think of it as a personal agenda or menu: there are many possible elements and combinations. There are fears to do with physical illness and incapacity, fears of being handicapped, of being a burden on friends and family, and fears of being unable to contribute to family life.

There are fears about physical pain: "How much suffering will there be and how will I stand up to it? What if I can't cope and show that I'm a coward? What happens if my family see aspects of me that I've always managed to hide from them so far?"

Then there are fears that are sometimes called "existential" fears, about the ending of life itself — the end of existence. And spiritual fears: "What happens afterwards? Will there simply be oblivion? Will there be an afterlife and could there be punishment?"

Then there are fears to do with the achievements of the person's life — concerns to do with dying while some of life's potential is unfulfilled, of not having achieved enough, of not having succeeded, and of not having made the best use of time. There may also be fears and concerns to do with rifts between family and friends — of fences that should have been mended some time ago and now seem to be irreparable.

And there are practical fears, of what may happen to the children afterward, what may happen to the surviving spouse, to the business, to the running of the home, and so on.

We shall consider how these fears can be aired in the later part of this chapter, but for now I want to emphasize that each individual has his own list of fears of illness and death. You, as supporter and friend, cannot know what is on that list unless you ask. If you help the person to talk about what is on that list, you will be giving an enormous amount of help. You may think that, like someone opening Pandora's box or a pressure cooker, you will be overwhelmed by what emerges. This doesn't happen. In the vast majority of instances, you will bring great relief by helping the patient discuss his pent-up fears. All you need to do is to allow the patient the time and space to ventilate what's on his mind, and to let him know that your friendship is steadfast, whatever his fear.

Hope, Despair, and Depression

Facing up to the possibility (or probability) of the end of life is a monumental task for the patient — it seems to be the worst thing that could possibly happen, and that once the hope of a long and healthy life is gone, nothing remains but despair.

Despair, like anger, fear, and denial, is a very common emotion throughout the stages of dying. No magic formula will instantly banish it. The word "despair" really means "the loss of hope." This might suggest that the only "cure" for despair is hope. The problem is that there are many different kinds of hope, and some (particularly false hopes about the outcome of the illness) can actually be *un*helpful to the patient.

Despair usually comes and goes in cycles. Like shock, despair tends to overwhelm the patient for a time, then fade, then return, and so on. The human mind is an adaptive system that does not function very well under extremes of emotion. Our minds are programmed to find a balance and to return to a normal state as soon as possible after an emotional shock. Very often, this adaptive mechanism works. This is how people are able to do such normal things as cooking immediately following major shocks such as floods or earthquakes — this survival mechanism is built into the way our minds work.

We often see, then, terminally ill patients facing despair in waves. Often after the despair has ebbed away, the patient tends to overswing into one or more hopes, some realistic, some not. Donald, an air-traffic controller, was a patient treated for a lymphoma affecting the brain. He and his wife, Eileen, were articulate and intelligent people capable of great insight. Donald described his mood swings as he went through the treatment: "Some nights I wake up in the absolute depths of despair. You told me that the chance of cure was small — well, at three o'clock in the morning, that means zero. Then a couple of days later, I find myself thinking that even if the chance is small, it may be me who is going to be lucky. It's not easy, but each time we talk it over, it gets a little bit easier."

This cycle is a very common way of adapting to the bad news. In most cases the depth of the lows and the height of the highs decrease, so that the swings become less violent and extreme. You should be aware of this normal adapting process. If your friend is in despair on Tuesday and optimistic on Wednesday, it doesn't mean she won't be feeling low again on Thursday. And if she *does* feel low on Thursday it doesn't mean she's mad, losing her mind, or manic-depressive.

While despair is a change in thinking, depression is a change in mood or in *feeling*. It is quite possible to *feel* depressed even when knowing intellectually that there is hope. In practical terms, despair is very often accompanied by depression, but not everyone who is depressed is in despair. It is extremely important to remember two things when supporting patients in despair or depression — first, both despair and depression come and go in cycles, and second, what really matters is how bad those cycles are.

Medically, the physical signs of depression include inability to sleep (usually waking in the small hours and being unable to get back to sleep), crying much of the time, loss of appetite and interest in conversation and interactions with other people, loss of facial expression, and particularly loss of smiling. Now I don't want to turn you into a doctor; all I want to do is to alert you to the signals of major depression. Severe and prolonged depression can be helped by medication, and if you are aware of the depths of the patient's depression you can call it to the attention of his doctor. Of course, symptoms such as loss of appetite or sleep may be the result of other causes, such as the disease itself, or uncontrolled pain. It is up to the doctor to decide whether the patient is going through major depression that will be helped by antidepressants or whether the patient's deep sadness is part of the adjustment process. Doctors' opinions may vary, but you can help best by checking that the doctor is aware of the problem. Many patients put on a brave face for the doctor and only reveal the genuine agony to relatives and friends. As a doctor I have often discovered the real situation from discussions with the supporting friends or family.

The medical team may well call in a psychiatrist to help the patient with severe depression. Needing the help of a psychiatrist doesn't mean in any way that the patient is mad or losing his mind. It's simply that assessing the depth of depression, judging how the patient is coping, and deciding what kind of help is required is a job for experts, usually psychiatrists. It is often difficult to judge how deeply depressed someone is. Distinguishing severe depression from a transient sadness requires great skill and experience. I spend a lot of my time looking after seriously ill and dying patients, and I still find I often need to call a psychiatrist to help me assess a patient's mental health. Often, the patient's first reaction to the possibility of asking a psychiatrist's opinion is something like, "First I get an illness, then I find I'm going to die, and now you think I'm losing my mind as well." With the many different kinds of therapy that are available, and the many different medications, one often needs expert psychiatrists to decide which will be the most appropriate form of help.

Before we finish considering the various aspects of loss of hope, we ought to think for a moment about the (often) false hopes of miracles and miracle cures that are very commonly raised by friends and family. Many people who were told by their doctors that they would have died years or months ago are alive today, and their examples are often cited to bring hope. Doctors are often wrong when predicting the survival of individual patients. I regularly have to admit that the only thing I'm certain of is my own uncertainty in matters like this. However, the major point of citing miracles is that if even one or two people have survived, apparently miraculously, then how can someone take the patient's hope away? Why shouldn't we just spend all our time and energy hoping or praying for a miracle and traveling from shrine to clinic to shrine for a miracle that might be just around the corner?

There are no simple answers to these difficult questions. We shall return to the difficult problems of confronting despair and desperate stories of miracles shortly. For now, the point I'd like to make is that human beings are often quite good at planning for the worst while hoping for the best. If you help the patient make plans for the worst and if something miraculous *does* occur, the only thing you've wasted is time and effort making unnecessary arrangements. If, on the other hand, you spend all your time together hoping that the disease will go away and it does *not*, the patient will approach death unprepared and overwhelmed by events.

Bargaining is another way the mind struggles with the threat of death. The patient may bargain in many ways. He may suggest a transaction between patient and doctor along the lines of, "If I agree to have the treatment, will you promise me it will work?" Bargaining may often be an internal pact made by the patient, in which he promises to change some aspect of his behavior (such as smoking, being bad-tempered, not spending enough time at home) as an offering to propitiate the disease. Bargaining may also take the form of a pact between the patient and his God: "Get me out of this, and I'll go to church every Sunday."

Bargaining is a battle between hope and despair. The patient is saying, "I partly accept that the disease is upon me, but I am only prepared to accept it if I can make it go away, and here is what I am prepared to do to make it go away." The bargaining mind accepts the news in small pieces, rather than being overwhelmed by it. Bargaining is not a stage of the dying process. It is the result of the struggle within the patient's mind between the reality of the situation and the forces of hope and despair.

To summarize, coping with your friend's despair is one of the most difficult aspects of supporting a dying person. It is often, in fact, the aspect that takes the greatest toll from the friend in terms of effort and (sometimes) exhaustion. In the last part of this chapter I shall suggest some practical ways of approaching this difficult problem.

Guilt

When anyone becomes seriously ill, guilt seems to accumulate everywhere. It seems to fall out of the sky like a sudden shower and it can be most destructive. It is not easy to define guilt, but the most consistent feature is the feeling of responsibility — whether or not it is justified. If my daughter falls into a swimming pool fully clothed (as she once did) I might feel guilty (as I did), and that guilt might be justified (as it was). If, however, my daughter becomes ill due to a random event, I might easily feel just as guilty, even though I am not responsible at all. At the center of any discussion of guilt lie two concepts: personal responsibility and punishment.

Guilt is such a common emotion because our society has deeply ingrained ideas of reward and punishment, and of responsibility. Everyone tends to feel guilty when there is a catastrophe such as a serious illness because our society is organized to expect that for every catastrophe there must be someone or something to blame. While there are considerable cultural variations within different societies, basically every culture has strong lines of responsibility running through its traditions and reflected in its laws. Think for a moment about the massive investigations that go on if there is an air crash or an accident at a factory or mine. The purpose of those investigations is to establish what happened, who is responsible, and to whom sufferers or their families can apply for recompense. This process is so much part of our social system that most of us accept it as a fundamental fact of life. Every society has some system of reward and punishment. These codes of reward and punishment are, in large part, what holds the particular group together, giving the individual members identity as part of the group as a whole.

While no blame for a *natural* disaster can be attached to a specific person or company, isn't it interesting that insurance companies call these events "Acts of God," as if some blame must be established rather than acknowledging that there is no blame at all? We are all brought up to look for the cause of calamity.

For a calamity so obvious as the threat of death we all have a strong instinct to allocate blame. The most natural consequence of this instinct is that the patient himself may regard the illness as a punishment for sins committed in the past.

To make matters worse, some diseases *are* caused by personal habits (cirrhosis of the liver can be caused by alcohol, for example, while cancer of the lung is almost always caused by smoking). The combination of these facts and the social atmosphere of responsibility and punishment make it very easy for the patient to regard the illness as retribution. In fact, apparently random punishment may actually *induce* an effort to find a cause where none exists. This recalls the school of parenting in which one randomly and periodically punishes children on the basis that if one doesn't know what the child has done wrong, it's a fair bet that the child does! This process of searching the past in order to find the cause of the illness is very common, and tends to be most pronounced when the illness is severe. I've seen very many patients who, upon learning of their cancer or multiple sclerosis or other major illness, felt a compelling need to identify something personal that had caused the illness. The system of reward and punishment does, at least, make some sense of the illness, whereas a completely random event unassociated with voluntary acts seems a senseless insult to the moral codes by which we live.

Whenever the cause of the disease is unknown or purely random the guilt reaction is, at least intellectually, superfluous. Of course, you cannot simply banish it by saying "Come on, you've nothing to feel guilty about." You must accept your friend's guilt as a normal and common reaction, even if it is not factually justified. However, where the patient's behavior *is* associated with the disease, guilt can be overwhelming. A young woman named Victoria developed lung cancer at the very young age of thirty-one. She had smoked heavily since the age of eleven and she was stricken with guilt about her disease. There was nothing I or anybody else could offer that would instantly abolish the sense of guilt, because everybody was aware that smoking causes lung cancer. What we did manage was to patch together a damage-limiting procedure. Her guilt had made her feel totally worthless, that all the effort and work she had put into raising her family and making a successful marriage counted for nothing. By stressing the real value of those relationships and by using her family to assist in the support we reduced the impact of the guilt feelings, although we could do nothing to remove their source.

Some people capitalize on the inherent sense of guilt. I once listened to a talk by a representative of a fairly well known alternative-medicine center in Britain that held the totally unproven view that every person's cancer is caused by the individual's psychological stresses. This representative said publicly that "the first thing we do when we meet a new patient with breast cancer is say, 'What is it that you have done in your life to cause your breast cancer?' " There is no evidence whatsoever that individual stresses do cause breast cancer, and I was *very* firm in pointing out that this was a guaranteed method of adding large amounts of guilt to the patient's already considerable suffering.

Thus, the first major cause of guilt lies in seeing the illness as a judgment or judicial sentence passed on the patient's previous life. The second factor that amplifies the guilt is the way the threat of death telescopes the future, putting a tremendous pressure on both patient and family.

By "telescoping the future" I mean that any life-threatening illness immediately reduces the time scale by which we all live. A sense of urgency magnifies any unfinished business. We all have unfinished emotional business, unresolved arguments with friends or relatives, aggressive or selfish things that we have done, actions in some way unworthy of the way we would like to imagine ourselves. While we are enjoying good health we may carry that list with us, assuming that we have sufficient time to sort it all out later. The threat of illness reduces that "later" to "soon." A sense of deadline arises. Suddenly, a person with a normal list of unfinished business is a patient with a limited future, and a sense of guilt about that unfinished business may seem to have arisen from nowhere.

People will, however, only feel guilty if they are sensitive about their actions and aware of other people's feelings and reactions. A person who upsets or offends other people with no intention of repairing the damage is unlikely to experience guilt. In the same way in which fear requires imagination, so guilt requires sensitivity. This neither compensates for the feeling of guilt nor abolishes the feeling, but is something worth pointing out to a patient you are trying to support. Guilt may not have a definite *purpose*, but it certainly does signal some positive qualities in the sufferer.

YOUR FEELINGS

Jonathan was a sixty-seven-year-old building contractor who developed bowel cancer that spread to his liver. It had progressed slowly over several years despite different treatments (including a lot of "alternative" medicines). He came to me for an assessment and brought his wife and daughter along for the consultation. It was immediately apparent that the three of them were experiencing different emotions. Jonathan himself was weary of the struggle and accepted that the end might be only a few months away. As sad as he was for himself, he tried to put on a brave face to spare his wife the pain of watching him suffer. His wife was distraught, but while she desperately hoped that something miraculous could be offered, she was preparing to accept the realities of the situation. She was moving away from her own anger toward acceptance of the situation. His daughter, however, was much more distraught. Angry, she cried often and would not allow anyone to talk about dying or giving up. As a result, the interview was exceptionally difficult, with much bickering among the three of them as well as a great deal of crying. I could only manage to point out to them that these important differences had to be faced without being swept away by talk of new treatments.

Jonathan's family experienced a variety of emotions arising from different sources. Perhaps we can consider the feelings that friends and relatives experience under three headings:

a. *Your "Sympathetic" Feelings*. You may experience feelings that reflect the patient's. The patient feels angry and you feel his anger, or he is in despair and your feelings reflect that despair.

b. *Your Feelings as Observer*. You may experience a range of emotions quite independent of what the patient is going through. For instance, she may have accepted the inevitability of death, while you may be angry; or you may be in despair while she remains optimistic.

c. *Your Feelings as "Target," or, Your Reactions to What the Patient Is Expressing*. This applies particularly to anger, which may easily be directed at you; but many of the patient's emotions will produce separate emotional responses in you, and we need to think about those, too.

The central component of any feeling that you as friend may experience is the sense of impending loss. It does not matter whether you are the patient's spouse, child, friend, or colleague, the severity of your sense of loss depends on the *closeness* of your relationship. By and large, relationships, however brief, are based on trusting and relying on one another. The threat of the end of the survivor's emotional investment means a great change in that trust and reliance. It also means the end of the survivor's emotional investment, the end of all that caring and all that mutual dependence. This painful concept will be, to some extent, at the root of your own pain.

Your Sympathetic Feelings

You will experience some emotions solely because the patient is feeling them. Whether the emotion is anger, depression, denial, fear, or any other (with the possible exception of guilt, which is almost always an individual's exclusive emotion), you experience it with the patient. Psychologists and psychiatrists draw a thin line between "empathy" and "sympathy." That sort of strict definition is not useful in this context. What is important is that when you find yourself angry or depressed or afraid, you ask yourself, "Why am I feeling this way?" If the answer is, "Because my friend is feeling this way," then you can focus on your *friend's* emotions. If, on the other hand, the feelings arise from something in your *own* emotional makeup and attitude, then you can be aware of this response so that you don't thrust or project your own reaction onto the patient.

What I'm saying, then, is that you need to recognize sympathetic feelings. These natural responses can almost always prove useful in supporting the patient.

Your Feelings as Observer

As a friend of the patient, but as someone who will survive him, you will have your own feelings about your friend's illness and threatened death. Not only are you entitled to have your own feelings, but it would be impossible for you *not* to have your own feelings about what's happening. The only important thing is for you to sort out, as far as you are able, which feelings *are* your own, so that you don't confuse them with the patient's feelings.

What, then, are the feelings you may experience? As an involved onlooker you will almost certainly feel considerable sadness about the impending loss. There is very little that anyone can say to reduce sad feelings, because the death of someone we love is, obviously, sad. It needs to be stressed that the part of you that feels the sadness is the part of you that cares, a part of your personality that's worth cherishing even while it is causing you pain. (As one commonly quoted phrase puts it, "The part that hurts is the part that counts.")

In addition to the inevitable sadness and pain, you may experience emotions similar to the patient's but which are yours exclusively. You may go through shock and disbelief of your own. Sometimes this might be transitory and slight ("I can't believe that my sister has cancer"), while sometimes it might be true denial ("Derek looks so well — they must have made a mistake"). This sort of true denial may cause problems. One couple, Susan and Bob, had a difficult time when Susan developed secondary symptoms after several years in remission. While Susan was able to accept the news and initiate pragmatic plans for their children, Bob could not. At first he thought he was helping Susan by his attitude (he kept on telling her that positive thinking could reverse the growth of the tumors). However, it was clear to me that Susan was being prevented from "unloading," and, in spite of the best of motives, Bob was putting an obstacle between them. We talked about this in some detail, and as Bob moved past his own denial to an acceptance of the situation, he became a source of support for Susan. A friend's own denial is not a rare phenomenon, and if you find yourself in that position, step back, look at your denial, and ask yourself who it is helping. It may be helping you, but, in most cases, it won't be helping the patient.

As you can see, while your emotions may often mirror those of the patient, oftentimes those emotions are yours exclusively. The key, in terms of supporting the patient, is to identify which are which. Before turning to Your Feelings as "Target," I shall now consider some of these differences.

Anger and Blame

You may experience anger of your own. The target of your anger may be (as the patient's may be) the healthy world, the uncaring universe, the unfairness of the system, the seemingly uncaring or incompetent health professional, or — and this is really important — you may be angry at the patient himself. Feeling angry at the patient *because* he is ill and dying is a common reaction.

It might at first seem peculiar that the friend would get angry at the patient, but it happens often. It is particularly likely when the relative is, in some way, dependent on the patient. In the most common situation the patient is the family's breadwinner and the supporter is the dependent husband or wife. What commonly happens is that the healthy, dependent spouse comes to resent the disruption of family life. She may have major fears about what will happen after the patient has died, and so becomes angry and often incommunicative with the patient *because he is the bearer and the representation of the illness, and the source of the disruption and threat.*

The fact that you understand and recognize the source of this anger will not stop it from happening. Ruth Gallop remembers very clearly a time when her husband, Leslie, was terminally ill, their son was very young, and they had to travel overseas. As Ruth put it, "I found that I was so angry that I couldn't talk to Leslie for a time." But why was she angry? And why angry with him? "Because by being ill, the sick person seems to be letting the healthy partner down . . . plans cannot be made, or if they are made, fall through . . . nothing seems sure or secure . . . and all the emotional investment you've made in the other person seems about to be lost." Ruth was already a skilled psychotherapist, and yet the load of anger she experienced was so heavy that it almost caused a communication breakdown between her and Leslie. Fortunately, she was able to talk to other therapists about the problem. Helped to see what was going on, Ruth was able to deal with her very strong feelings, and to start talking normally with Leslie again.

Ruth's experience is not a rare one. A spouse may resent the disability of the sick family member very intensely. His reactions may seem cruel to the outsider. Relatives and friends of patients may, for example, be slow in bringing painkillers, visit the hospital rarely, or deny the patient signs of caring and affection (including sex); all with excuses that vary from the plausible to the flimsy. These are not signs that the friend doesn't really care; rather, they're outward signs of his anger and resentment. I've seen these reactions very often. Here are just a few examples of what some friends and relatives have said:

"This is not what I agreed to take on when I married him."

"Why can't she be healthy again?"

"He's doing it deliberately."

"She's not trying anymore."

"He's enjoying the attention."

"I have to work like a slave, and he gets all the sympathy and attention."

"All my life I've been looking after someone. First it was my parents, then my children, now it's him. When is it going to be my turn to have someone look after me?"

These feelings are neither unnatural nor (usually) untrue. Healthy, you may well find yourself greatly resenting this illness, which you *didn't* expect and *don't* want, which *is* destroying your relationship and your life-style, and which *is* simply unfair and unjust. There are so many reasons for resenting illness, the threat of death, and loss. The real problem is that very often the patient, who seems to be the cause of all the resentment, becomes the target.

Naturally, understanding the causes of your own feelings of resentment doesn't wipe them out at a stroke. But if you are able to recognize some of these feelings in yourself, you may be able to think them through in your own mind and talk about them with other people (including, perhaps, the patient). Once you get a handle on your anger, instead of having it overwhelm you, you can get on with supporting the patient. You may, with enough perspective, see that it's the disease, and the awful impact it has on the relationship between you and the patient, that is the cause of your anger. If so, you'll see that the patient should not be your target.

Of course, real anger may be almost impossible to check. You may find yourself exploding in anger or resentment, and saying things that later seem unfair and unkind. The best thing to do in those cases is to think about what you've done or said, go back to the patient once you've cooled down, and try to describe what you were feeling. Veronica, a woman in her late forties who was nursing her elderly father, found that her patience reached its snapping point because of his incessant and fussy demands. After one of his worst complaints, she dropped his tray on the floor and ran out, slamming the door. An hour later, once she'd cooled down, she went back to her father's room "to explain how I felt but not to apologize or to reopen the argument." Her straight, cool explanation achieved a good deal. She and her father agreed that he would make his demands more reasonable while she would try to meet as many of those demands as she reasonably could. So, even if your feelings are far from "good" or "beneficial," it is much better to talk about your anger. Try to help the patient understand the reasons behind your outburst, rather than simply letting such an incident pass unacknowledged, a potential block between the two of you.

Another reason relatives blame the patient for the illness is to shore up their own hope that it cannot happen to them. We all hope we're not going to get ill ourselves, and we constantly look for things that the patient did wrong that makes the disease "her own fault." The implication is that if we, the onlookers, don't make that mistake, we'll be all right.

When I developed the condition that made me so ill — an inherited autoimmune problem not caused by anything other than being born with certain genes — people very close to me took the opportunity to give me lectures about everything I'd always done wrong. Everybody had a diet plan I should have followed, a sleeping pattern I never learned from, bowel training I studiously ignored. The relatives that gave me these lectures spoke out of a genuine sense of love and concern, along with an added sense of fright and shock that this could happen to someone so close. It was the latter that pushed them into looking for reasons why the illness should have happened to me and not them. I must add that this moralizing, however well intentioned, is very boring. The last thing a patient wants to hear is what he should have been doing since birth to avoid getting ill.

Limit your advice. When you are close to someone who is ill, do not make his plight worse by burdening him with your views on how he should have lived his life. It may make *you* feel better but it won't help him at all. It may well distance you from the illness, and thus bring you some relief, but it will also distance you from the patient, which makes you less of a help.

Of course, some diseases *are*, directly or indirectly, caused by what the patient does. Smoking causes lung cancer (or 97 percent of it anyway), for example, while prolonged excessive consumption of alcohol causes liver damage. But if you want to help your friend, do not lecture him on the causes of his disease. Don't use the weakness of the patient's position for any self-righteous teaching. It will not be helpful, and even if it is correct, it is too late.

Fear

Of course you will have your own fears. The precise nature of those fears will partly depend on the nature of your relationship with the patient. You may be frightened of being left alone, of being helpless, of cracking up and failing to cope, of being a hindrance to the patient afterward.

You may have very vivid fears of being left isolated, of never having any real life after bereavement, of going mad without her. Or you may have very practical fears about what's going on at present. What if the illness carries on for a very long time, until you are both exhausted and drained and come to resent (or even hate) each other? However shameful these fears may appear to be, most friends and relatives have them. They're neither unnatural nor a sign of some callous streak in your personality.

Sometimes as the patient comes to accept death, the friends or relatives become more frightened, rather than less so. Deborah was a very beautiful woman in her late thirties whose very aggressive melanoma (a rare type of skin cancer) had relapsed. Her husband, Harry, was an extremely pushy man, and although the situation was hopeless, he simply was not ready to accept it. Deborah, however, *knew* she was dying, and she wanted to talk. Harry would listen to anything she said, except on the subject of death. She wanted to hear the truth and talk about it; he didn't want the facts out in the open. Deborah had some important things she needed to say to Harry, and she asked if I would help.

The interview, at first, threw me completely. Every time Deborah started to talk about the fact that she was dying, Harry stopped her, physically. First he pushed her fruit juice at her and put the straw into her mouth. Then it was a sandwich. When she continued to try to say she knew it was the end, he started kissing her on the mouth while she was still talking. His behavior was so out of the ordinary that I was as embarrassed as Deborah. But it occurred to me that Harry, for all his strength, was scared. He was very frightened of Deborah's impending death, and the fact that she clearly wasn't frightened made him feel even more ill at ease. Once we started talking about what *he* was afraid of, things got much easier.

Harry was so used to pushing everybody else around that it was hard for him to face up to the fact that even he could be afraid of certain things. But having fear is a common enough reaction, one that you can watch out for in yourself. Try to recognize your fear as honestly as you can. This recognition is the first step toward control of the fear that may be driving your anger and your frustration.

Therefore, when you get feelings of fear, you should ask yourself, "What is it precisely that I am afraid of?" Try to assemble a list of the things that you most fear. Some are things that may happen to the patient and some are things that may happen to you. The more closely you look at your fears, the less dreaded they will appear. Of course, no amount of thinking can ever abolish fears entirely. You are going to lose your friend, and that, in itself, is something unknown and fearful. But these exercises can reduce the scale of the fear, making it easier for you to better help your friend.

Guilt

A friend's guilt is partly caused by the same mechanism that makes the patient feel guilty; death is a punishment for which you must have committed a crime. However, you may also feel that you have not been as close a friend or relative as you might have been. Both reasons are common and powerful. And both can be given expression as anger.

I remember one patient's son whose burden of guilt was the driving force controlling his behavior. The patient, Ivy, was in her late sixties when I was first asked to see her. She was seriously ill, but there was a good chance her tumor would respond to chemotherapy (which it later did). She was an immigrant from Eastern Europe and she "had a certain way about her." She was incredibly stubborn and obstinate, and had a strong desire to be in control of everything. Even though my description doesn't make her sound so, she was, at heart, a very endearing woman who, once she was sure I understood who was boss (i.e., her), accepted me easily. The problem was her son.

Bob was in his early forties, and was as he told me in the first few seconds of our interview, a "big-shot lawyer." Our interview started somewhat stormily. He gave me a combination of the Spanish Inquisition and the Headmaster's Speech to the Wayward Pupil. My knowledge of cancer treatments was probed in detail. I was made to understand that I would answer to Bob for anything I did wrong. I listened to Bob work himself into quite a state of anger. Then I asked him how he got along with his mother. I told him that I found her quite difficult to understand and to get along with. I made it very clear that I was certain Bob had been a good son, and that she was probably quite a difficult mother and at times apt to criticize. Once Bob realized that I wasn't going to criticize him the way his mother always did, and that I didn't think he should feel guilty about his mother, he relaxed, and the big-shot-lawyer facade faded. He told me quite openly that he was very used to being shouted at (which is why he was shouting at me) and that he had been feeling very guilty about his mother and her illness. Could it have been detected earlier if he'd visited her more often? In this case, the answer was no. Would the treatment have been easier if she'd been living with him? Neither for her, nor for him. Should he have been doing more? No, because however much he did, she would always express herself in terms of dissatisfaction. But this in no way meant he was a bad son. In the end, all three of us got along very well. She was quite happy grumbling as long as we respected her; Bob was happy as long as we knew he was really a good son; and I was quite glad that nobody was shouting at me.

Sometimes the relatives actually feel more guilt than the patient. Often, that feeling of guilt merely reflects the state of the relationship prior to the illness, and that is the way things will continue during the stages of dying.

The sense of guilt is heightened by the spotlighting effect I mentioned earlier. We are all used to having arguments and then resolving our differences. But if one day that row is followed by the onset of serious illness, we are likely to feel very guilty. Curiously enough, the people who are likely to feel most guilty are children. If a parent is taken ill, the children may feel that it's because of something they did ("Maybe if I'd always tidied my room like Mom said, she wouldn't have died and left me"), and this is something that I'll explain in greater detail later on.

Finally, you may feel guilt because you are going to survive and the patient is not. This sensation, sometimes called "survivor guilt," is predictable whenever we are threatened by the loss of somebody very close. It is most intense when the patient is the child, but in many relationships the relative or friend feels guilt as a powerless bystander. This, too, is a normal reaction to impending loss.

Your Feelings as "Target"

We can now consider your own feelings, not as an observer of the patient, but as the target of the patient's emotions. It is always hard to be supporter and target at the same time. Your friend is going through a series of different emotions, some coherent and understandable, some contradictory and reflexive, and at various stages they may be directed at you. So, while you are trying to support and help the patient and trying to stay close, you may well be the target for some of the patient's moods and feelings. The closer you are, the more likely you are to be on the receiving end of his emotions.

You may be the target for anger because you're healthy and you're going to survive his death. You may be the target for denial, if the patient can persuade you to join him in pretending the illness doesn't exist. You may be the target of guilt, since people who are feeling guilty can often superficially reduce that feeling by making other people guilty. And you may be the target for despair — the patient may use despair as a weapon to beat you. You may be asked, or compelled, to witness anger directed at other people, and you may be dragged in to referee and to take the patient's side in any dispute. All of these things can happen, and all are hard on you.

The key to being an effective supporter of the patient is maintaining a balance between staying close enough to the patient to understand her experience, and maintaining enough distance so that you do not trade blow for blow in direct confrontation. That balance is easier described than followed. You can make it a little easier for yourself if you try to imagine the patient's feelings. For instance, Veronica (the woman nursing her fussy father) told me that when her father reacted to her rearranging his pillows by shouting, "Will you stop bugging me!" she felt she had two choices. "I could have shouted right back at him and told him he was a cantankerous old man — or I could tell him I realized how awful it felt to be in bed, without being able to do things for himself. I just didn't want to have an argument, so I used the second approach. And suddenly, we weren't having an argument — whereas, before, we always had. It was extraordinary."

So, if your friend gets angry and tells you to get lost, even in the heat of the moment when you most feel like doing precisely that, try to think to yourself: "Why is she being like this? What is she going through?" You will often feel enraged, frustrated, or desperate, and from time to time you will hit back. It is impossible to alter your every response. But, by being aware of the possible options, you can reduce the number of situations that degenerate into confrontation.

In summary, then, what I've been trying to do is to help you unknot the strands of your own feelings — where they come from, and what they mean. If they originate from the feelings of your friend, it will be helpful to be aware of that so that you can concentrate on him. If they are your own feelings about what's happening to your friend, then it is important to know that too. If they're helpful emotions, you can share them; if they're unhelpful, you can try to filter them out. And if your feelings are reactions to being the target, then you need to be aware of that too, so that you can support instead of fight.

A GUIDE TO GIVING SUPPORT

Supporting someone coming to grips with the threat of terminal illness involves both practical and emotional help. Support can bring a sense of cohesion to a family whose members may have grown distant from one another over the years. Freda, for instance, had always been the strong one of her family, while her husband, Joe, and son, Robert, had always been quiet and shy. Frightened by Freda's illness, Joe had withdrawn, and Robert had become angry and sullen. The four of us made a real effort to understand the various obstacles that were keeping them all apart. While they had been divided for some time, they very much wanted to strengthen their family bonds. The immediate threat posed by Freda's illness helped focus their desire to function as a strong family. After much hard emotional work, things changed quite remarkably. The family became so close that when Freda became bedridden, she asked to be looked after at home, something all three had initially feared. There she remained until the end of her life, well supported and well cared for. Afterward, Robert and Joe were both justifiably proud of themselves, and of Freda, and felt that the closeness they had all experienced at the end had helped Freda die feeling a greater peace.

At the stage of facing the threat, the major impact of the illness on the patient is emotional, and it is in that way that your support can be most useful. You can, and should, offer practical as well as emotional support, even early in the process. Offers of practical help carry an emotional and symbolic value for the patient. The following guidelines may help you offer effective emotional support at the early stage.

General Guidelines

1. *See Where You Fit In*. Do not rush in and take over. Go cautiously at first to find out where you can be of greatest help.

2. *Expect Variability*. As I have mentioned already, your friend's mood and outlook will change from day to day. This is neither his fault nor yours. If you expect it, you will not be put off balance when it happens.

3. *Expect Repetition*. People coping with major psycho-logical stress often feel the need to go over the same ground time and time again. If you can, go along with it.

4. *Following the Patient's Agenda, Not Your Own*. Rather than starting your support with a program already estab-lished, feel your way and improvise. It is often not helpful to visit a friend with a list of things she "simply has to do," whether that list includes faith healers, relaxation tech-niques, new diets, or anything else. See what the patient is already doing before you step in with your plans.

5. *Do Not Equate Activity with Support*. Many times the things you *do* for the patient will be helpful; sometimes things you do not do are most helpful. Do not, for in-stance, spend time getting second and third opinions unless the patient wants you to help provide them.

6. *Become Informed — But Don't Become a World Ex-pert*. This is a guideline that will be repeated in later chap-ters. It is extremely important that you learn enough about the medical situation to help constructively. Do not, how-ever, become an expert in your own right, catching the patient in a conflict of opinions.

I have already outlined approaches to some of the emo-tions you will encounter. The following additional guide-lines are directed at specific responses.

Helping with Denial

Supporting someone who is going through denial is not easy. You are caught between two difficult choices. If the patient is ignoring obvious signs of the serious nature of the disease, and asks, for instance, "I'll be better in no time, won't I?" your options may seem limited. If you support a statement that isn't true, this will lead to trouble when the patient doesn't get better. If, on the other hand, you say, "No, you won't be getting better," you immediately cast yourself as the patient's adversary, a person who takes away hope. Furthermore, by attempting to answer the question, you're also (subliminally) allowing yourself to be set up as an authority figure, which will make life even more difficult for you later.

The first point to remember is that denial is powerful. You cannot simply override the patient's denial by force of facts. This does not mean that you have to accept openly his interpretation of the situation. There are ways of exploring the way someone is feeling without attacking him. For instance, you can try a "what if . . ." approach, thus allowing the patient to think about the *possibility* of not getting better, in the abstract. You can also ask about the medical facts. Your supportive conversation might proceed as follows:

The patient says something like:

"I am going to get better,
aren't I?"

You have several choices:

You could say:

"Of course you are."
— a direct response that
will reduce your
credibility when
things don't go well
later.

or

"No, you're not."
— a direct response that
makes you appear cruel
and adversarial.

Or you could say:

"What have the doctors
told you?"

or

"I hope you will, but it
might not happen."

or

"I'd like that, but perhaps
we ought to see what
happens."

All of these leave
open the possibility
that things will get
worse, and allow
you to continue to
be supportive.

They also allow you
to raise the question,
later: *"Should we*
make some plans for
what to do if you
don't get better?"

Helping with Despair

Remember that "despair" means loss of hope. Remember also that, while a cure and the return to a healthy life may not be yours to grant, there are realistic hopes that are in your power to offer. The single central principle of coping with someone's loss of hope is that you should never rush in to fill the vacuum with false hopes. Promising things that cannot be delivered simply weakens your credibility as a friend and supporter. You will appear less reliable, and your friend may be discouraged from trusting you and leaning on you later, when she may need you most.

1. *Stick as Close to Reality as Possible.* You should never promise anything you think will not happen. Patients often say things like, "I feel awful — things have to improve soon." These statements cry out for an optimistic reply, and it seems almost unnaturally cruel to deny that plea. But promising things you can't deliver will simply make you appear to be untrustworthy in the long run. By telling a person that something is "not mine to promise" (a phrase that I find useful in clinical practice), I let him know that I would *like* to be able to make him better, that I hear his *hope,* but that I am not unrealistic and that I have limitations. It allows me to be honest and realistic without seeming to withdraw from the patient, and without appearing to crush all hope.

2. *Acknowledge the Way the Patient Feels.* Allow her to say how rotten she feels. Listen to it, accept it, and *be* there — stay close. If you can't think of anything to say, it may be because there's nothing *to* say. Just stay with her. Hold her hand if you don't feel awkward, or put your hand on her arm or shoulder. You can't fix or banish

despair, but simply staying with the person during the worst of it, rather than withdrawing or recoiling, is one of the most helpful things a friend can do.

3. *Reinforce Genuine Hopes.* There are hopes that can be achieved once the patient realizes that you have accepted and understood her despair. It is possible to relieve pain in at least 90 percent of patients with cancer. Knowing that, you know that hoping for relief from pain is realistic, a feasible goal. It is also realistic to hope, in the great majority of cases, that the dying person will be able to maintain his or her dignity and respect. This is often a major concern of the patient, and it is important for both of you to know that this hope is realistic.

Most important, as relative or friend, you can promise that you won't abandon the patient. You can tell the person that no matter how rough things get, you will be there. This is one of the great comforts you can offer. Most patients have a great fear of being abandoned near the end. In a recent film made by a young woman dying of AIDS, she said, "Most of all, I don't want to die alone." The hope that you'll stay by the patient is a vital one you can make real.

So far, I have discussed the initial shock of the diagnosis and the ripples that spread out through you and the other members of the family and circle of friends. Now I shall move on to consider the impact of the illness as it continues — the feelings that go along with "being ill."

6

Being Ill

It is not easy to define precisely the "being ill" stage. This is the period of time after the initial shock of diagnosis, but before the patient (or the friend) really *knows* that the end is near. In other words, this stage is the stage before the patient accepts the *inevitability* of imminent death as a reality. As I have already said, human emotions don't divide themselves neatly into stages. This second stage can begin very soon after diagnosis (or even before, if the patient has felt ill for some time), and may go on to the end of the illness, if the patient never truly accepts his imminent death.

This phase is characterized by two major factors — illness and uncertainty. The uncertainty is painful in itself, and the constant fluctuations of hope and despair can be very wearing on the patient and friends. As the English writer Michael Frayn wrote, "I can stand the despair. It's the hope I can't bear." The main features of this phase are that the threat of death is so prominent (but not imminent) in the patient's life and the illness is materially affecting the quality of that life.

THE PATIENT'S FEELINGS

As the illness progresses, all the emotions that we discussed in Chapter 5 continue. While the major shocks may fade as adjustments are made, minor new shocks spring up, particularly if new disabilities or symptoms develop. Denial becomes a bit more difficult (though some patients will maintain it nonetheless) and depression becomes more common.

We can best think about the patient's experiences in this stage by splitting them up into two kinds: first, the physical symptoms caused by the disease; and second, the impact of these symptoms on the patient's life and emotions.

The Physical Illness

Serious illnesses vary to a vast degree. Some advance rapidly, paralyzing the patient and quickly rendering him incapable of most independent activities. Other illnesses may, in the early stages, cause no impairment of function at all.

Most people have an image of a serious or life-threatening illness instantly rendering the patient gravely ill and totally incapacitated. Although this does infrequently happen, the patient's physical condition usually deteriorates gradually, or in stages. So, it's important for you to realize that this deterioration takes place over an unpredictable period of time.

Many patients will feel fairly well at the time of diagnosis. Many serious diseases develop relatively slowly, and nowadays, most people consult doctors early, rather than ignoring symptoms for long periods of time. Feeling well while you know you've got a serious disease is a difficult state to accept. Although, obviously, it's good not to have major physical symptoms, and good to be able to perform a reasonable range of daily activities, this feeling of wellness often makes it very difficult to come to grips with the seriousness of the situation. As one patient put it to me: "I can't seem to get my mind round it." Patients often say, "But I feel so well." Even more frequently, they express their frustration when well-meaning relatives and friends say things like, "But you look so well!" "It's as if," the patients say, "I have to *prove* to them that I've got a serious illness."

This early period *can be* beneficial, in that it gives friends and family time with the patient — time that can be utilized to the fullest. But it can also be somewhat baffling, like a "phony war" that makes the illness and the threat of death even more unreal.

This early part of the illness may last for some time. The patient's condition will generally deteriorate by degrees. As one elderly woman put it, "I've gradually changed from a person to a patient, haven't I?" Some of the many possible physical problems may develop, and if they happen to go away temporarily, they don't go away "properly," and the patient is never allowed to forget them totally. This feeling of having to face the continuous threat or presence of physical symptoms is what I call "the grind of being ill."

The Grind

In describing the "being ill" stage, many patients have told me that their illness takes on a sort of physical presence in their lives, like an unwanted and uninvited guest sitting at the dinner table, making normal life and conversation difficult and strained. My own experience, even though it lasted less than two years, taught me how quickly the illness becomes (quite literally) "part of the family," and how quickly serious physical symptoms such as pain, loss of appetite, and nausea can drain the color out of life, leaving the patient (and family) in a sort of sallow, monochrome world.

It might be worth your trying the following mental exercise to get an image of what "the grind" is like for, say, a terminally ill patient who has the nondescript, but very common, experience of simply feeling ill, lousy, or fifth-rate, of suffering from (to use the correct medical word) "malaise." Think for a moment about what it feels like when you get the flu. You know that second-day-of-flu feeling, when you feel simply rotten, when everything hurts or is uncomfortable, and when you can hardly do anything. Getting up for a cup of tea or a visit to the bathroom is a major undertaking, and you could hardly imagine doing both of those things in the same hour. We have all had that, and felt very sorry for ourselves, but we have also known that the feeling would pass, and we would be back to normal in a week.

Now imagine that this second-day-of-flu feeling does not go away, and you are feeling just as bad at the end of a week. Imagine how you would feel at the end of the second week. Then imagine it for a month. A month goes by, and you are not back at work. Nobody can tell you when you're going to get back to work, or if you will go back at all. Now add to that a regular series of tests: X rays, blood tests, scans, and perhaps treatments with drugs by tablets or injections, or radiotherapy, or surgery. On top of that, there may be all the uncertainty about the future. . . .

I am not suggesting that you perform this mental exercise as some form of scare tactic. I am trying to get you to visualize the presence of chronic illness, and the continued frustration that most patients experience, and which so many families and friends never really understand.

During this phase, support from friends and family is often at a premium. When the shock of the diagnosis is new ("Isn't it terrible, Brian's just been told that . . .") friends and family may well flock around with welcome sympathy and support. But as the illness continues and nothing much changes, friends and family do tend to fade away into the background. Nothing much seems to be happening to the patient. The need seems to be less urgent. But, the fact that nothing seems to be changing does not mean that needs are less; in fact, it is often the opposite. One patient, an elderly man with lung cancer, told me, "It's a vicious circle — my son doesn't come to visit, so I get depressed, then when he *does* come to visit I'm all depressed and angry, so naturally he doesn't enjoy the visit and doesn't come to visit so often. So I get more depressed and more angry — and then I don't blame him for not coming to visit. I wouldn't if I was him!" In this grind phase, the patient and the family and friends may *all* get bored and frustrated. You need to be aware that this is a common and normal feeling at this stage.

To summarize then, the most important aspects of the physical illness (after the initial shock) are: the loss of control and the loss of daily activity; the wearing, grinding effect that this causes when it doesn't get better; and the uncertainty about the future.

The Emotional Impact of Physical Symptoms

So far, I have been building up a picture of some of the physical feelings your friend may be experiencing. But there are many other ways in which the illness can affect your friend's quality and style of life. I shall mention some of them briefly. A complete list, however, would be impossible to compile, first, because there are so many kinds of physical problems, and second, because the impact of any given physical problem depends on that person's previous life-style.

Let me explain that in greater detail. If I broke a leg and needed to wear a plaster cast for a month, that would be an irritating nuisance. But because I am not very athletic, and because I could just about manage my job in medicine, it would not be a disaster. If, on the other hand, I was a professional tennis player or an actor, it *would* be a catastrophe. In practice, the impact of the illness depends on the way the patient arranges his priorities. (In my own case, for example, when it seemed quite likely during the two years of my illness that I would not be able to walk easily again, it was not difficult to investigate subspecialties of medicine that could be done sitting down. In arranging for that possibility, I wasn't being brave, I was just acknowledging that I wasn't totally dependent on my physical abilities.) Ask what is bothering the patient most of all about his physical situation, for his answer may not be the same as yours were you suffering from the same illness.

As another example, consider an operation for breast cancer. Depending on the size of the tumor, the size of the breast, and several other factors, the patient might have part of the breast removed ("segmental mastectomy," sometimes also called "partial mastectomy" or "lumpectomy"), or the whole breast removed. The impact of the operation varies enormously. There may be a very serious change in the way the patient thinks about her body. She may no longer feel sexually attractive. She may be reminded of the diagnosis each time she undresses. The operation site may frighten her; it may frighten her partner; and either or both of them may become depressed or anxious. The way in which one particular person reacts to the operation will depend on her personality — on the way she thought about her body and her image before the illness. Was she very self-conscious? Did she set a great deal of store by her physical appearance? Her sexuality is another factor. Is she secure, or does she constantly need to be reassured that she is attractive to different people? Her closeness to her partner and friends, and her openness about things that bother her, or her reticence and her tendency to put on a show of being just fine; all these routines in existence before the illness will set the pattern for the impact of this operation on the individual person.

The reactions may surprise you and even the patient herself. Barbara, who was in her early forties at the time of her mastectomy, said, "I was upset by the way my body changed — but even more than that, I was upset *that I was so upset*. Sure, I'd always taken a pride in my appearance, but I didn't realize that it mattered so much, and in such a deep way. That surprised me — and I didn't like what it told me about myself. Wilf [her husband] didn't seem to think about me differently — he was wonderful, but there were times when I was even more upset *for him*." It took a lot of time to sort those feelings out and restore a balance.

It is very difficult to make accurate statements about the impact of an illness or an operation on an individual. You might think, for instance, that the smaller the mastectomy, the less the impact. In fact that is not the case. Detailed psychological testing on patients who have had partial mastectomies showed that these women can feel as depressed and as deeply upset by the operation as women who have had the whole breast removed.

The varying reactions to mastectomy offer but one example of the emotional impact of physical symptoms. A colostomy (an operation in which an opening from the bowel is made in the abdominal wall, requiring the patient to wear a drainage bag) may upset many people. There may be problems with appearance and self-consciousness. The more fastidious a person is, the more he may be upset by not having total control of his bowel movements. If the patient has a long-term partner, a colostomy may not affect their sex life at all. On the other hand, if the patient is single and has had several shorter-term relationships, a colostomy could drastically affect that life-style.

Loss of hair, which accompanies several kinds of chemotherapy and radiation to the head, often considerably upsets patients. One young man with Hodgkin's disease said, "Losing the hair was the worst bit because that's when I had to stop pretending there was nothing wrong with me. It was when everybody had an excuse to ask me what was wrong." There may also be, depending on the disease and the site of the problem, walking difficulties (requiring a cane or a wheelchair), a catheter (a thin tube put into the bladder to drain urine when the bladder does not work properly), pain, difficulty in breathing (perhaps requiring oxygen by mask or tubes in the nostrils), difficulty in eating, difficulty in talking (with diseases of the larynx or vocal cords), and many other symptoms.

The key to understanding all of this is that your friend

is facing up to something he can't completely control. He cannot have complete control over the physical symptoms. This will upset him to a degree that depends on how much he *values* his ability to control everything in his life.

In summary, then, the physical illness is as individual as the person it affects. What matters most is discovering what is actually going on with your friend right now. What bothers him the most? How close are you willing to get? If you are willing to work closely with your friend, then you will have to confront certain common reactions to the overwhelming presence of physical illness. Perhaps the most important of these is the feeling that it is all hopeless, and that there is no point in even trying to carry on.

"What's the Point?"

Most of us are surprisingly courageous when it comes to short-term immediate emergencies. Even people who think they are not good at putting up with pain are often unexpectedly good at coping with it when they have to. However, a lot depends on what we make of the situation confronting us. Generally, our ability to cope with pain is quite good when we think it will not last long — when the pain is the short-lived kind, such as that associated with a healing operation scar, a broken limb, or childbirth, for example. When, however, there is no recognizable end to the suffering in sight, it is much more difficult for the patient to muster strength and willpower.

The terminally ill patient may often ask, "What's the point in carrying on?" A patient speaking to an audience of doctors at an international conference said, "It's like a tunnel that we are asked to crawl through — except that when we've crawled all the way through it, all there is waiting for us is another tunnel, and more tunnels after that."

This reaction is extremely important. It is a complex mixture of emotion and reason. It may contain some despair, a feeling of lost hope, but it may also contain a genuine and rationally developed balance sheet of the costs and benefits of struggling against the disease, a recognition that there really is not much to be gained by continued struggle. You, as supporter of the person going through the illness, must take such assessments seriously. There's no single word to describe this deep and chronic "what's the point?" feeling, but it is neither an acute, short-lived despair, nor a sudden suicidal urge to end it all. It is a gradual, eventually total, *darkening* of that person's view of the world. The light goes out and the picture becomes ingrained with a pervasive gray. This is very hard on the family and supporters. They often feel (quite rightly) that they're doing their utmost to brighten up the picture for the patient, who has now gone sullen on them without appreciating their efforts.

There are no simple answers to this very serious kind of doubt. You cannot fix it or banish it instantly. But you can use the same approach that I mentioned in dealing with despair in the last chapter: acknowledging and accepting the depth of your friend's feelings, and reinforcing those hopes that are realistic.

For the moment, then, let me summarize what the patient may be experiencing in the "being ill" phase: the continuing emotions that began in the "facing the threat" stage are compounded by the emotional impact of the physical illness and uncertainty about the future. These emotions will, of course, rebound to you, so let us now look at some of the things you may be experiencing.

YOUR FEELINGS

Now that you have an image of what the patient is going through, we can start thinking about you. During the "being ill" phase there is a greater chance that your feelings will be out of step with the patient's feelings. It is during this stage that major differences and gaps may develop between you.

Your Sympathetic Feelings

As in "facing the threat," you may easily pick up on the patient's feelings. You may find that you experience her anger and her frustration. You may also find yourself thinking that there really is no point in carrying on.

The message here is the same one as in "facing the threat": you have to be aware of where these feelings originate. If what you are feeling is a direct reflection of your friend's experience, then it will help you to realize that. It will not instantly cancel out the intensity of your feelings, but it will help you get them in perspective. For instance, if one day you are feeling really low and going through a "what's the point?" phase, you might feel so bad that you don't want to go and visit your friend. If, when you think about it, you become aware that your reluctance stems from your last visit, when your friend was in this state and you picked up on it, then you may feel better about visiting. By noticing that your feelings didn't actually start with you ("she's feeling really low, and that's what's making me feel low"), you may be able to give yourself a bit of space and gain strength and stamina.

Your Feelings as Observer

In the "being ill" phase, your reactions to the illness may be very intense and may create deep rifts and obstacles between you and the patient. "To be totally honest," a relative once said to me, "the most awful thing about a long serious illness is that it's frustrating, it's boring, and it's a drag."

Everybody feels resentment and anger at some stage during a friend's serious illness, particularly if it lingers for some duration. Angry thoughts and feelings occur which, in the cold light of day, seem cruel and callous. Here are some examples of what relatives and friends of some of my patients have said about this phase:

"I don't know whether I can stand it any longer."
"I can hardly bear visiting him anymore."
"It's getting to the stage when I almost wish she were already dead."
"I seem to hate him because he's not getting better."
"I've got my own life to live, you know."
"I can hardly wait for it to be over, but that makes me feel terrible."
"This is no kind of life we're leading."

Supporting a seriously ill person takes a major toll on the supporter. Your life-style may be affected as much as (or even more than) the patient's. You may be spending your time doing things you don't really want to do. You may resent that the burden of the relationship may have fallen on your shoulders.

You cannot help but feel resentment. But you can help (both yourself and the patient) by recognizing that you do feel some resentment and by not pretending that it does not exist. If you understand that you are feeling this way, you can respond to the patient by saying something like, "This is really tough and I'm getting very bad tempered" (which is a way of *describing* your feelings) rather than "You never do anything except lie there and grumble" (which is a way of *exhibiting* your feelings, and quite likely to lead to an argument).

You may have a sense of "anticipatory grief," feelings that anticipate the patient's death and your resulting loss. I will deal with anticipatory grief more fully later.

You *will* probably resent the loss of your independence, you will feel the weight of the demands made on you, you will miss the fun you used to have together, and you will resent the illness. All these feelings are very common. You should try hard to separate the resentment that you feel toward the illness from your feelings for your friend. Unfortunately, the patient is often the only person around to catch the blame. He is also the embodiment of the illness. It is easy for you to shift the focus of your resentment and unhappiness straight onto the patient, adding to his problems as well as your own. Being forewarned is being forearmed: aware of that tendency to shift your feelings onto the patient, you can reduce its impact.

A GUIDE TO GIVING SUPPORT

In the "facing the threat" stage, the emotional shock is massive. In the "being ill" stage, the problems are both emotional and physical. The sick person now needs help on two levels: practical and emotional. It is always worth remembering that there is more than one way of offering help and support. For instance, if your friend is deeply depressed about hair loss from chemotherapy, you can certainly be kind and supportive and constant. You can also, on a more practical level, help her get a wig. So, before we start looking at the tactics and approaches, let me state clearly that the first thing to do is to find out what the major trouble spots are, and whether any of them can be fixed simply.

1. *Assess the Needs.* There are hundreds of booklets available to patients and their families covering the details of, for instance, care of a colostomy, managing catheters, mastectomy counseling, walking aids and chairs, aids for daily living, and so on. If you want to help your friend in some specific way, there are sources of information, including the doctor and nurses looking after the patient, the local cancer society, disease-oriented self-help groups, local information offices, and local hospital volunteers.

2. *Help Your Friend Make Choices.* The physical and practical support is vital, and usually much appreciated, but on the emotional level, things are often difficult. The "being ill" stage almost always involves choices and decisions for the patient. He may have to decide whether to undergo a course of treatment, whether to get a second opinion regarding surgery, or whether the side effects of therapy are tolerable when measured against the potential benefit. And you may be asked to support him as he faces up to these vitally important decisions and uncertainties. It is crucial that you accept that the patient has *the right* to make his own choice. You must respect his choice, even if it does not coincide with your opinion. You can help him balance up the pros and the cons, and you can help him realize that he does have a choice. But you cannot, and you

must not, choose for him. If you do, you will line yourself up for blame as one responsible for the outcome. It is often hard for family members to allow the patient freedom of choice. Often the pressure for a patient to persevere with treatment comes from the family, who do not themselves have to go through the side effects.

Ben was in his early forties when he was diagnosed as having a cancer that was particularly resistant to therapy. His doctor was fair and honest and made it clear that drug treatment had only a small chance of helping him. The situation was tragic, but, to make it even worse, he and his wife had only just started a long-planned-for family. Their daughter was only a few months old. Ben did not wish to go through a course of treatment that was most likely to be ineffective. He did not want to be made ill by the therapy during what might be his last chance of spending time with his daughter. His wife, and some of her relatives, felt differently. Ben was pulled in different directions. He told the doctor, "I think I've got to have the chemotherapy for my family's sake." But this decision clearly made him unhappy and uneasy.

His doctor, working together with John Martin, brought the family together to talk about it. After a lot of discussion, the family realized that because their desire for Ben to live was so strong, *they* weren't ready to accept that he really was going to die, and that treatment really would not prevent his death. It was hard and painful for them to accept this, but when they did they realized that they had been putting unfair pressure on Ben, and that it was his right to make his own decisions.

In this example, it was quite hard for the family to accept Ben's right to choose. But if they had not done so, and if Ben had been a weaker person, he might have gone through treatment unwillingly, "for the sake of others."

He would have resented those "others" for making him do it. Instead, Ben and his family realized how much they all meant to each other, at a time when that love was most crucial.

3. *Explore What Your Friend Really Wants and Means.* Often during treatment, a patient may say something indicative of a deeply felt fear or anxiety. Think for a moment about the following, relatively common situation. Richard had a tumor in the bowel which was diagnosed at a time when he felt physically well and had relatively few symptoms. The X rays showed the tumor and his doctor recommended surgery, which would result in a colostomy. Richard said to his wife: "I'd rather be dead than have a colostomy." What did he mean by that?

The answer is that he may have meant several different things — and some of those meanings may actually have been contradictory. He may have meant "I'm not ready to face the fact that I have cancer of the bowel." This common emotion employs thinking along the following lines: "The doctor says I have a serious illness and need surgery. If I don't have surgery then I won't have to face the fact that I've got this disease." In other words, refusing surgery is a way of denying the existence of the disease.

The statement may also be an expression of fear. Sometimes patients cannot admit to being scared, so they say something that sounds quite brave: "I'd rather be dead . . ." has overtones of "I'm not afraid of death," when actually the fear of dying has pushed them into this pose.

Richard may also have meant that he genuinely and sincerely loathes the prospect and inconvenience of surgery and a colostomy. He may earnestly wish that he didn't have to have it, and may think that he can abolish it from view by comparing it to something even bigger, that is, his own death.

The words may also be expressing the patient's anger. Rage and rejection of the concept of a colostomy may be his way of raging against the disease. By rejecting the offered treatment he at least exercises some form of control over his situation, thus compensating for the fact that he has no control over the disease itself.

His statement may also be a cry of despair, although that is less common. Read literally, "I'd rather be dead than have a colostomy" seems an expression of despair. But by reading between the lines, you will probably see that the patient does not want to die. In practice, despair is only rarely the central important component of this sort of exasperation.

You can help the person in this crisis identify the strands of his feelings. Get him to talk about what he means by what he's said. Does he really mean he wants to die? Or does he mean he's afraid? And, if he's afraid, what of? Dying? Surgery? Inconvenience? Pain? Or does he mean that he simply can't face the decision now? And if that is the case, does he *have* to make that decision today, this minute? Does he have a few days or a week to decide? Does he need more information? Would it help to talk to the doctor some more, or to someone who's had the operation, or an expert who can answer the detailed questions?

"I'd rather be dead than have a colostomy" is not, then, a single, monolithic statement that you have to accept or confront head-on. It's an emotional response that may contain a lot of different elements. By staying close and encouraging the patient you may find the truth behind a topic that you might previously have thought totally unapproachable.

7

The Last Stage

In the last stage of a terminal illness, the patient may come to recognize the inevitability of death, and accept that it is going to happen in the immediate future. Some patients accept it early in the illness, and some never accept it. Similarly, among health professionals, some authorities feel that patients *must* accept it, while others feel that patients don't *have* to accept it openly, but that it is generally better for them and their friends if they do. One of my patients — Gillian, a woman of forty-one — said to me, "I think it's very important that I say good-bye to you. I think I'm going to die very soon, even though I was hoping it would be much later." The next morning she spent a long time on the phone with one of her two daughters, and the other daughter and her husband were with her that afternoon when she died. What struck me about Gillian, in addition to her obvious courage and insight, was that she used every minute available to her, right up to the end of her life, to keep emotional contact, to get support from, and to give support to her family.

But what about you? What should you do about accepting the inevitability of your friend's death? When is it permissible for *you* to think that it's time to stop struggling and time to prepare for the end? When should you stop asking other people about miracle cures in Mexico and special clinics in Switzerland? When is letting go permissible, rather than a sign that you don't care? And what happens once you've let go?

Answering those questions is the main object of this chapter. I shall start by talking about what acceptance means to the patient, and then about what it means to you. In the third part of the chapter, I shall consider some of the difficulties that occur before acceptance (including the need for second opinions and alternative medicines), and then look at the major factors that need to be considered after acceptance, such as the patient's last wishes, the living will, promises that you feel you ought to make, and what you may feel if you are not there at the final moment. Finally, I shall deal with the issue of euthanasia.

THE PATIENT'S FEELINGS

As acceptance grows (if it does), the patient usually feels sad and, very often, tender. Once the major uncertainties and the big struggles are considered over, there is usually more peace and less anger. By definition, in the final emotional stage, denial has disappeared.

Acceptance almost always brings true sadness (as opposed to depression). The patient is sad at the prospect of being parted from friends and family, and about leaving the enjoyable things of life. This sadness is natural. You should allow the patient to express this sadness candidly, although this will make you feel sad as well.

Although sadness is most common, not every dying person feels that way. Some people with strong religious beliefs and a firm image of an afterlife face the final stage with no sadness at all, instead looking forward to being reunited with those who have died before them. This belief creates an enormous comfort. These patients are generally very strong about facing the end of their life, and are able to communicate easily with their friends and family.

For most other people, sadness will be a central part of the final stage. The sadness itself contains grief. Many people are, at the end of their life, mourning for themselves. They don't want to stop living and so they mourn, in exactly the same way the surviving relatives will mourn after their bereavement. If you realize that this is a normal, rational part of the process, you won't be upset when you see it.

It is crucial to remember that most people die as they have lived. If, in your daily life, you're an easy and cheerful person, then you will probably approach the end of your life in the same manner (provided you are kept free of pain or other major physical problems). If, however, you are a neurotic or cantankerous sort, then that is probably the way you'll be at the end. Deathbed conversions are rare. Most of us, of course, are mixtures — a bit neurotic, a bit brave, a bit humorous, a bit grouchy — and most of us will meet our deaths with the same mixture of moods or traits.

Some deaths are so much in character that they seem to exemplify the person's life. One such death was that of my favorite uncle, Barry, who was simply a great human being. He was funny and bright. He had a strong sense of social justice, he was good at his job, and everybody in the family loved him. He had a quick temper, but was equally quick to forgive and forget. He died young, but even in the last few hours of his life, he showed great care and concern for all of us around him, and was appreciative of all the help we had given. I don't want to sound overly sentimental, but his death was an exceptionally profound experience for all of us. His last words were a joke. It was actually a very witty comment on something that was going on, but the real point is that, at the very end of his life, Barry behaved as *himself*. I have never forgotten that. In fact, it was as I watched Barry cope with dying that I understood that death can happen with dignity and integrity. It's a goal that we can try to help our friends to achieve (and to achieve ourselves when it's our turn). Barry was Barry until he stopped. He gave all of us with him the courage to try to do the same.

It should be your objective as friend and supporter — as it is my objective when I'm looking after dying patients — to help your friend let go of life *in his own way*. It may not be your way, and it may not be the way you read about in a book or magazine, but it's his way and consistent with the way he's lived his life. You can and should help your friend achieve that.

There are some medical details of the last hours of a patient's life which may be of help to you. Most people die by slipping into a coma before the moment of death. It is not invariable. Some deaths are sudden, a few are violent, and a few are painful until the very end. The great majority of people, however, will slip into a state of unawareness in which those around them can't get through. This phase may encompass the last few minutes or hours before the death or, in the case of brain damage or similarly debilitating problems, it may go on for days, weeks, or months. The type of death portrayed on television or in films, in which the dying person is totally coherent one instant and dead the next, is rare.

Many survivors of near-dying experiences (including Dr.

David Livingstone, whose famous account chronicles his near death from a lion attack) have described a sense of peace and tranquility that comes as death appears to be close, a calm that removes pain and struggle. It appears that this sensation is actually caused by substances produced in the brain called endorphins, which are similar to a naturally produced painkiller. It also seems that many of the "depersonalization" experiences recounted by near-death survivors, in which they felt themselves moving outside their own bodies, believing that they observed events from a remote position, are caused by lack of oxygen in the brain section known as the temporal lobe. Similar experiences have been produced during certain special kinds of brain surgery in which the patient needs to be awake.

The end of life is quite often imbued with a special tenderness. Although deathbed transformations are not common, and a J. R. Ewing usually dies as a J. R. Ewing, rather than a Saint Francis of Assisi, quite often patients become more sensitive to their own emotions and to those of the people around them. It is almost as if their ability to receive emotions improves, as if their "emotional hearing" was suddenly sharpened and heightened. Usually this is not a *new* side of their personality appearing, but rather an increased emphasis on the sensitivity already present. When this happens it is good for the patient and the family.

YOUR FEELINGS

As in the earlier stages, you may experience periods of quite intense sadness and anticipatory grief, as well as anger and resentment. But in addition, as the illness moves into the final stage, many relatives and friends experience emotional and physical exhaustion. Sometimes, at moments when it seems that you and the patient will be locked in this pain forever, you may feel a sense of impatience. One patient, Anne, who had been married to her husband, Peter, for over twenty years, told me about her feelings during his prolonged illness. Caring for his physical symptoms had Anne always running up and down the stairs of their home. She put her feelings this way: "One day I thought to myself, 'if you call out to have your pillow fixed once more, I'm going to hold it over your face — I can't take this for one more day.' "

Anne's frustration sharpened into a sense of impatience; a common feeling for those people looking after a dying person. Naturally it seems cruel and callous, but thoughts such as, "I felt that if he wasn't dying, I'd kill him myself," are quite common. It's like having a baby that cries all the time. Most parents faced with a baby that won't stop crying say, or think, "One more minute of this and I'm going to hit this child." Almost every parent feels like that at some time, and yet the number of parents who *do* hit their babies is very small. At some time, almost every supporting relative has thoughts of impatience, and anticipates the end of the patient's life with some sense of relief. In the vast majority of cases, those thoughts are normal reflex reactions and not a sign that you've stopped caring forever.

Loss of Control

You may also experience a loss of control. Many of the things you have done for the patient may have been valuable and appreciated, but as the patient nears the end, you may feel the strong disappointment of losing control as the disease takes over. This feeling of impotence and frustration may show itself as anger or withdrawal. You may subconsciously blame the patient. You may withdraw from her because it seems that so much of your emotional investment has been wasted. Veronica (the woman with the fussy father) said she became aware of her rising resentment as her father became more ill, "because at least when he was eating the meals I cooked — even though he grumbled — he allowed me to be useful. I had something to do. When he couldn't eat, I felt useless. And I kept feeling that all the cooking and preparing I'd done before had been a complete waste of time." Again, being aware of these feelings and their causes may allow you to step back and take a break, so that you can look at the whole situation in perspective again.

Differences in Acceptance

What happens when the patient reaches acceptance and is preparing himself for dying and you are not able to accept it? This difference in acceptance can create major difficulties. Victor, in his late twenties, had a particularly aggressive form of liver disease, which had been diagnosed about a year before I first met him. The family was South American and very close. His mother was distraught at Victor's declining health. Her distress was made much worse because she depended on translators to tell her what doctors and nurses were saying about his condition. Victor and his sister were both highly intelligent and well educated. Victor, however, was resigned to the fact that he was going to die, and his sister was not. She took him to an alternative-medicine clinic and smuggled the drugs back with them on the plane. She continued to give him the drugs, even during the last few days of life. Victor was too ill to care very much about this and when John and I asked him about it, it was clear that it didn't disturb him greatly.

Two days before he died, Victor asked for a priest to give him the last rites. His sister and mother refused to allow this. It was an exceptionally difficult situation. They had no *right* to refuse him this sacrament, but on the other hand, a screaming argument on the ward around a dying man was something we wanted to avoid. We discussed it at length with them. We pointed out that the most important person was Victor. We gave the family the space to express how much they wanted him to live. We pointed out that the last rites do not, in themselves, hasten death, but that denying him what he wanted was unfair and cruel. After much discussion, they relented and, in so doing, were able to reach a state of acceptance similar to Victor's.

Bear in mind that you do not always demonstrate how deeply you care by taking action. Sometimes the best you can do is accept the patient's illness as fully as she has. Victor's sister took him to the alternative-medicine clinic, in spite of his own wishes, because she was not ready to accept his death and she thought that this would show how much she cared. Later on, we all agreed that there were other ways of showing her love. Just being with him was enough.

As you can see, in the final stage, acceptance is the most important factor in deciding what you are able to do and how you are able to support your friend. Accordingly, I'm going to divide this part of the chapter into two sections dealing with issues that arise before acceptance and those that come up later.

HELPING THE PATIENT
BEFORE ACCEPTANCE

When you *know* that the end is near, sadness and anticipatory grief are natural and have a healing effect. Very often, however, you *don't* know when the end is close. Wondering whether to help the struggle for life or to encourage acceptance of the death is a dilemma for relatives and friends.

To help resolve this dilemma you should attempt to answer two questions: first, what are the medical facts and second, what choice does my friend wish to make in these circumstances?

The medical facts are not always easy to establish. The situation is most straightforward when the doctor looking after your friend commands her trust and respect, and has fostered good communication between the two of them. When a respected doctor says that active treatment against the disease is no longer possible, and that the objective is palliative care (meaning control of symptoms), acceptance is easier for all concerned.

The difficulties arise when the patient — or you — have doubts about the inevitability of the patient's death. You may *not* have a doctor you respect ("Does he know enough to be sure there's no hope?" "Has he heard of Professor Smith in Chicago, who's apparently a world expert?"). Other people may put doubts into your mind ("There's this neighbor who had cancer just like Joe's and it was in his liver and the doctors said it was hopeless but he tried treatment X or Y"). When I was ill, for instance, I received dozens of letters from well-meaning people who had seen me on television. They sent me all kinds of miracle cures, including names of faith healers, and magnetic, copper, and herbal things to wear or to sleep on.

So, concisely stated, the dilemma is as follows: is the illness genuinely terminal and do you believe your friend's doctor? Or do you keep on trying until the very last instant? I want to make an observation from my medical practice, and then to offer a way of picking a path through this tricky area.

First, more suffering is caused by desperate struggling than by apparently premature acceptance. When I made a television program about a laetrile clinic in Mexico, I saw many patients who were desperately ill. Some were so ill that they were not even allowed into the clinic but were "turned around" in the parking lot. But many had made the long trek from their homes, at considerable expense in time, effort, and money. Desperate, they were concentrating entirely on being cured. They were often angry, often wildly optimistic, and very rarely at peace. They spent very little time being close to their spouses or friends.

The attitude that leads patients to "go anywhere and try anything" has a price tag. The price is the loss of time to be close to friends and families, and the loss of tenderness and sensitivity that might have been allowed to grow.

Hence, in considering the medical facts, you balance two emotionally laden scenarios. If you accept the medical fact that it is hopeless, you might miss out on the probably minute chance of longer life for your friend. If you don't accept it, you may very well be helping your friend waste time and money when both are in short supply.

My suggestion is that if the patient is really in doubt, or if you are in doubt and the patient accepts your view, get a second opinion. Ask another doctor. But if the second opinion is the same as the first, and you then have the feeling that you *must* go seek a third, and maybe a fourth, until you hear what you want to hear, stop and think. If that second opinion agrees with the first and you *still* feel desperate, ask yourself, "What am I unable to hear?" Constant shopping around is a sign of denial. It's a sign that the patient, or you, or both are not ready to accept what's happening.

There is a story about a famous doctor who was the editor of a prestigious medical journal. He developed a tumor for which there was no effective treatment. As part of his work, he daily read dozens of academic papers on various aspects of medicine. So now he called on experts in the field from all over the world to give him advice. Most told him that nothing much could be done for the disease itself, and that control of symptoms was the best to hope for. But he kept asking more experts and spent more and more time at it, until a friend of his recognized what was going on and said, "What you need is a doctor." His friend meant that he needed to rely on one person whose opinion he could trust and whose recommendations he could follow with confidence.

Much of a patient's attitude in the final stage depends on trust, and that's a very personal bond between doctor and patient. If your friend does trust her doctor and can accept his advice and guidance, you should support that relationship. It is a valuable resource for her. If that trust is not there, you should discuss the possibility of finding another doctor. The doctor-patient relationship is personal and subjective, and, almost like a marriage, it depends on matching the personalities of the participants rather than on any absolute qualities of one or the other. Your friend needs the best match available in the circumstances. A perfect match is rare.

In summary, then, something apparently miraculous *does* occasionally happen as a result of shopping around. Unfortunately, in the great majority of cases *nothing* miraculous happens, and time, energy, and opportunity are lost. Despite the cries of "How can you give up on him?" from well-meaning friends and advisors (who may be unable to accept the patient's death themselves), acceptance of the inevitable and preparation for death is neither cowardly nor treacherous.

Alternative Medicines

As I have said, it is often in this last phase, before acceptance, that the alternative-medicine treatments are discussed. The availability of these treatments significantly affects your feelings and your ability to support the patient. Most alternative, unconventional, medicines have a brief vogue and then disappear forever. Usually they rise in popularity very rapidly over one or two years, ride the crest of a wave for five years or so, then fade.

The hallmark of alternative-medicine practitioners is that they do not try very hard to find out whether their treatment actually works. They do not follow up with their patients. They do not collect information to find out if they're curing 50 percent, 10 percent, or none at all. They do publicize and they do make claims.

I have met many of them, and all the ones I met were sincere, kind, and caring. There may well be charlatans and rogues around, but they are a rare and minor part of the problem. The central difficulty is that most of the

alternative-medicine practitioners are "good with people"
but not good at treating diseases. They are almost always
good listeners, charismatic, and intuitive psychotherapists,
all qualities of a good doctor. The condemnation and
persecution they suffer at the hands of more conventional
authorities simply adds to their charm and mystique.

Sadly, they usually lead their patients on (often uninten-
tionally) before abandoning them in a worse state than
when the patients first visited. Hopes raised and then
dashed do more damage than hopes never raised at all.

As a "conventional" physician I often have to care for
patients after they have exhausted much emotional effort
and some money on alternative medicines. Often they feel
angry. Laura was an immensely rich and successful woman
who had spent six months receiving useless therapy. She
was enraged with the practitioner who had virtually de-
luded her into imagining that the treatment was helping.
However, she was even angrier with herself. She — who
had always been so decisive in her business and personal
life, who had never had difficulty assessing other people's
value and credibility — had been conned because the
threatening illness had destroyed her objectivity. Like
many such patients, Laura would not even write a letter to
the practitioner (let alone take legal action) because she felt
so foolish. For this reason, many such practitioners carry
on in their field never realizing that their patients are paying a heavy price for false hopes.

You should, therefore, think about why the patient — or
you — wants to give it a try. If you try an alternative
approach with very little expectation and very little expen-
diture of time or money, little will be lost. If your effort
becomes a major project with hopes raised high, then do

be careful. If no miracle cure arises, you will both be worse off than you were before you started.

Practically speaking, it's worth checking a few points. How long has the clinic been going? How many patients have undergone this treatment? What happened to them? How can you find out what happened — are the results published anywhere in a respected journal? Or is it all hearsay? What happens if the treatment doesn't work? Will it do harm? (The answer with alternative medicine is virtually always no. Nearly all alternative medicines are harmless.) What does it cost?

Resolving these issues may take a lot of time and discussion. But once they are resolved, and once the patient is genuinely resigned to the fact of dying, communication patterns between you will change. This is a time when you can be of major help and support.

HELPING THE PATIENT
AFTER ACCEPTANCE

At some point then, whether or not your friend tries alternative medicines, there will come a time when the struggle is over. To help you communicate at this important stage, I'd like you to try another mental exercise. Imagine yourself in the patient's position. Imagine that you knew today that you would not be alive in, say, three months. This is not an easy thought to entertain, but try to think now of what things would reduce your fears and anxieties, and make it easier for you to face up to the end. What sort of specific things would they be?

In general, two kinds of support would be most valuable: practical support in sorting out the details of your life (what one might call your "last wishes"); and emotional support to reinforce the idea that dying doesn't rob your life of meaning, reassurance that you won't be forgotten by the people that you have known and who survive you.

Last Wishes

When you and the patient are close and both know that he is going to die, you can help with the details. Help get the will sorted out. Help locate important documents. Find out whether the patient wants you to contact anyone (so many people have cousins or old friends that they haven't spoken to in the last umpteen years). If the patient has specific views about the very last phase of the illness, help him. He might want to be transferred to a hospice or to a palliative care unit or to another place specializing in support of the terminally ill, and you can help him find the right one. If he doesn't have a specific location in mind, perhaps you could contact a social worker to explain more, or you could get information from a local hospice.

Quite often the patient wants to die at home. Most people who like *living* at home probably want to die there if they can be reasonably comfortable physically. Many families are a bit horrified at first, and are worried about whether they'll be able to cope with the physical and the nursing needs. Home care is a great service to the patient if you can manage it. If, however, you cannot manage, then stop and get help. If you do your best and you can't manage it, you need not feel guilty. Most patients understand that their families have tried.

An alternative to home or hospital care is admission to a hospice or palliative care unit. Such units are devoted only to the care of patients at the end of life, and usually have staff who are highly trained and experienced in the control of patients' symptoms. Generally, such units have a higher nurse-to-patient ratio than a general hospital, with fewer doctors. In all of the units that I have visited, there has been a high level of support for patient and family, with backup from many areas including social work, chaplaincy, physiotherapy, and so on. Most palliative care units allow and encourage patients to spend days out with their families. Fears of a "one-way ticket" are rarely justified. Most units also encourage potential patients to visit the unit before admission to get the flavor of the place. This valuable introduction to the unit can greatly reduce the patient's fears. You should ask the social worker associated with the doctor looking after your friend for details of the local unit. It is often useful for you to visit the unit first and report back to your friend.

Other specific details may be equally important to the patient at the end of life. Does she have specific ideas about funeral arrangements? About organ donation? About cremation? If so, don't shy away from talking about them. If you say something like, "Oh come on, there's no need to talk like that," you isolate and frustrate the patient.

Often the major block to communication will be the relative or friend, and not the patient. When I was in my first year of medical school I was asked to pay a social call on my aunt's friend, a man in his early fifties called Alan. I only visited him twice, but we got on very well. He was good company and a great conversationalist. On the second visit he invited me to his party. He looked very ill and I was a bit confused. He said that he was planning a party for after his death (in other words, a wake) and he'd be glad if I went to it. I was very inexperienced at that stage of my career, and I became very embarrassed. I didn't know what to say. I didn't go to the party after his death, but I've often wished that I had had the equanimity to accept his invitation, and to tell him I would attend. While arranging one's wake is not yet accepted social practice, it does happen, usually successfully. The great choreographer Bob Fosse recently left a large amount of money in his will for some of his friends to enjoy a last dinner on him. Last wishes like this may cause you some pause when first suggested, but in helping celebrate the patient's life they may help him let go of it.

Sometimes the patient's wishes may appear a little incongruous. Three times in my career I have been involved in caring for patients who wanted to be married within the last few days of their life. In each case the patient was a man, and in each case he had been living with or had been involved with the woman for many years, while for various reasons they had never gotten around to getting married. Although the wish may have seemed odd at first, all three occasions were special, with the weddings taking place on the ward in a private room. In the third case some of the relatives expressed doubt about the marriage, but we pointed out that it was the patient's wishes that counted, even though immediate family was important to both spouses.

"No Heroic Measures" — The Living Will

Another area where you can be of very real and practical help is in assisting the patient to make his views on treatment clear to the doctors looking after him. Many people nowadays have very firm ideas of what they will and will not consent to in the way of hospital treatment when they have a terminal illness. Most hospitals in the United States and Canada have a policy of asking patients who are terminally ill whether they wish to receive cardiac resuscitation if their heart stops suddenly (an event called "cardiac arrest"). Many patients feel quite strongly that they do not wish to be resuscitated (an effort almost always unsuccessful with terminally ill patients) and they do not wish to recover consciousness in an intensive care unit with tubes in their lungs and veins. If your friend has similar views, make sure that the doctors are aware of them.

One device which has been of enormous value recently is the "Living Will." This is a short document signed by the patient and witnessed by you or another friend or family member, stating that the patient doesn't wish to have heroic measures carried out to prolong life if she becomes incapable of indicating her wishes. The document has legal standing in forty-one states of the United States at present, and in the others is certainly regarded as evidence of the patient's wishes. In some cases, doctors have been threatened with legal action for assault if they persevere with aggressive treatment in contradiction to a living will. A typical example of a living will is included in Appendix A of this book.

Most doctors — myself included — find a living will very helpful in hospital care of the patient. The document clarifies the patient's wishes and removes the ambiguity and uncertainty which might otherwise confuse care. If you know your friend wants this, try to get her a living will. In the meantime, help her make her views known to the doctor.

These, then, are some of the most important practicalities of the final phase. We may now consider the emotional support of a patient who has accepted his imminent death.

"You Won't Be Forgotten"

I'd like to return again to the experiences Ruth went through near the time of Leslie's death.

Shortly before he died Leslie became very anxious about his son, Michael, who was then less than three years old. As he and Ruth talked about it, Ruth realized that what Leslie was really saying was not, "Please don't let Michael forget me," but rather, "Please don't forget me yourself." Once that became clear to both of them, Ruth was able to tell Leslie how she felt about him at that moment, and about how she would keep an image of him alive for Michael in the future. I'm sure that Leslie knew that Ruth could and would do that, and her assurances made him less anxious.

Ten years later, Michael was confirmed in the same temple in which Leslie had been confirmed. Ruth said of Michael's confirmation, "There was something to do with continuity there. Even though Leslie had died, something was being kept alive, and Michael was aware of it. It was very special."

In my own case, the time during which I was told that I might die lasted only a few weeks and, as it happened, the doctors were never *sure* that I would die. Nevertheless, the thing that I most wanted to believe and to know was that the people closest to me would not forget me, and that we had achieved some things that would count after I had died. Some people gave me the feelings that there was worth in our relationship, and I still love those people dearly. As a patient once said to me, "There's one thing you can say about dying — you certainly find out who your friends are."

If you help establish the kind of continuity that Ruth

showed with Michael, and if you can show the person facing the end of his life that his value doesn't end, you are being a true friend.

I'd encourage you to talk about these things, even though it may seem awkward at first. Tell him that he's not lost to you, that he is still loved, and that you are not the same person you would have been had you never met. Tell him, because you may not have the chance later.

"I Want You to Promise . . ."

There are some demands you cannot meet. There is a social tradition that if a dying person makes a demand of you — a promise or a commitment — you are obliged to honor it, come hell or high water. Failing to honor a deathbed request or promise seems to carry a huge burden of guilt. My favorite example is from *Middlemarch*. The heroine, Dorothea, is asked by her husband, Mr. Casaubon, to promise to complete his life's work, a stunningly boring and instantly redundant commentary on the Bible. She says she'll think about it, and he dies that night, miraculously saving her from a life of pointless scholastic drudgery.

But you *might* be asked to promise something to which you would not agree in normal circumstances. What then? The best way to respond is to think about how you would reply were the patient *not* dying. Obviously, agreeing to a promise that is totally out of character ("I want you to promise to bring the children up as pickpockets . . ."), or to something that contradicts a central principle of yours, is not acceptable. In those circumstances, making a false promise will hurt you afterward. If, however, the promise is one you might ordinarily *try* to keep, then make the promise and do not feel unduly guilty if you do not manage to maintain it for the rest of your life. You are *allowed* to change after bereavement. Personally I think nothing is sadder than a bereaved person living, for instance, in a large and inconvenient house because "Dad would have wanted it that way." And when the family pleads with Mom to be kinder to herself, she says, "We all have our crosses to bear." But didn't Dad change his mind about things sometimes, when he was alive? And if he did, why should his widow have to live her life by a rule book written at the time of her bereavement?

"What If I'm Not There When He Dies?"

One of the most distressing questions a friend can pose himself is, "What happens if I'm not there at the moment he dies?" The distress caused in survivors absent at the time of death can be severe and painful and may last for many years. Why is this?

The answer is complex, and sorting out the various strands that make up this powerful and deep feeling is not easy. Let me first reiterate the medical facts. Most people are not conscious at the time of their death, instead slipping through a period of increasing drowsiness to stupor (as it is called), coma, and then death. The timetable is variable, but as a general rule most people are not actually conscious at the last moment of their lives.

Even so, many patients would like someone very close to them to be present at their death. Often the relative or friend specifically asks to be called if the patient's condition deteriorates seriously. Despite this, sometimes the friend wants to be but cannot be there, and feels badly about it afterward. There are often good and obvious reasons why the friend couldn't be there: the medical staff was involved in active resuscitation measures, the deterioration was very sudden and unexpected, or the friend lives too far away. The reasons are not very important. The point is that the survivor is frequently overwhelmed with guilt and grief.

It happened to Ruth that way. Leslie was giving a lecture in another city, Chicago, when he felt feverish and took himself to the local teaching hospital (he was on a course of chemotherapy at the time). An infection had developed in his blood and by early that afternoon he was dangerously ill. Ruth got a message to phone the hospital and asked if she could speak to Leslie. The nurse who answered the phone replied, "You can't speak to him now — he's dying."

Ruth says, "I still can't think about that without reliving the pain. I rushed to the airport to get to Chicago. There was a storm and no flights were leaving. I sat in the airport waiting for three hours. And when I got to Chicago, Leslie had died. The pain was massive — more than anything I'd ever felt before, or since. It was so bad that even now, seventeen years after Leslie died, I can't go back to Chicago without the whole thing, all the pain and all the misery, coming back to me."

But why is this last moment so important — or rather why do we think it is? Why is it so central that Ruth finds it painful even to talk about the subject nearly twenty years later?

Some of it is due to the sense of abandonment ("He died alone"). But there is more to it than that. In some ways we think that the last moment of life summarizes the whole of that life. It feels as if the fact that someone dies alone negates the many years of companionship that preceded the patient's death.

I think this is because we imagine that the person who has died is locked into the state in which he died. If he died alone, say, in 1973, then we tend to have a strange feeling that he's still alone in 1983 and 1993 — each and every time we remember and think of him.

This, of course, isn't true. What is stuck is our *memory*, and that is *our* problem. Missing the last moment of life is painful because of the way our memories are constructed. But years of marriage, friendship, and caring are not wiped out by the last few moments, however painful they are to recall later.

Euthanasia

The word "euthanasia" simply means "dying well" but there is a great deal of confusion about what it implies. Most authorities recognize two types of euthanasia. "Active euthanasia" means giving the patient a substance which will kill him. This is illegal in every Western country and is regarded by the judiciary as murder. There are no legal cases in which a person assisting in this act, and tried for it, was found not guilty of murder, although sentences have been reduced because of mitigating circumstances. No country has passed a law allowing active euthanasia. The main problem with such a law is the abuse it might foster, and the difficulty of devising a system of administering life-ending drugs. Although many people wish that there was such a law, at present there is none, and I doubt whether there will be a change in the foreseeable future. One country, Holland, has a different climate. Even there euthanasia is illegal, but it is estimated that each year between seven thousand and ten thousand terminally ill patients have their lives ended at their own request by their doctors. Even so, legal reform to accommodate active euthanasia in Holland is thought to be a long way off.

"Passive euthanasia," by contrast, means using normal drugs to keep the patient comfortable even if that usage might shorten the patient's life. This is perfectly legal and is standard practice on palliative care units, where the quality of life is valued. As a matter of fact, even though major painkillers *might* — in theory — shorten a patient's life, usually they don't, and some very detailed research in British hospices during the 1970s has shown that patients on narcotic painkillers live the same length of time as patients at the same stage of illness who are not on narcotic painkillers.

The use of effective drugs to relieve pain and other symptoms is the central objective of good palliative care. The living will is one of the ways in which the patient can demonstrate clearly his wish to receive this care. It is a humane and considerate way of looking after someone in the last stage of life.

8

Saying Good-bye:
The Function of Grief

So much has been written about grief and bereavement that it is difficult for anyone to see the forest for the trees. In this chapter, I summarize the central function of grief, explain how it works and how it sometimes goes wrong. I shall divide the subject into three broad areas. First, I'm going to talk about grief itself — what it does, what it is supposed to do for you as the surviving friend or relative, and the stages of grieving. Second, I shall deal with the anticipatory grief most people feel before the patient dies. Finally I shall consider the important problems that occur when grief doesn't do what it's supposed to do.

THE FUNCTION OF GRIEF

Grief is all about letting go and saying good-bye. By letting go of her attachment to the person who dies, the surviving friend becomes able to make attachments to other people in the future.

Losing someone close to us hurts a lot. It hurts because important ties are broken, ties that meet our needs, and that meet the needs of the patient. Generally, we let only a few people that close to us, so that when we lose them, or realize that we might lose them, it is those ties that bring us pain. Grieving normally reduces the hurt.

If, at some point in the future, you are able to be happy and fulfilled and make intimate ties with someone else, the grieving process has achieved what it's supposed to do. The person in whom grief *doesn't* do its job will often end up being unable to invest emotionally in anyone else again. (Like Miss Havisham in *Great Expectations,* who kept her wedding dress and cake preserved as they were on the day she was jilted — a perfect example of totally arrested grief!)

Remember: whether you wish to or not, you *are* going to survive the patient's death, *and that should not make you feel guilty*. It may well be that you would give anything to change places with the patient (particularly if the patient is your child) but that is not in your power. You have to face up to two facts, both of which seem awful at the time: your friend is going to die, and you are going to survive. Neither his death nor your survival is your fault.

At various times, you may feel (as many relatives have said to me) that life does not seem to be worth living afterward. This feeling is common, natural, and powerful. It cannot be rubbed out with a few phrases like, "you'll get over it" or, "life must go on." But an understanding of grief and grieving will help you to remold your life later on, and will allow you to traverse the grieving period (without trying to fight it or cut it short) in such a way that you emerge psychologically healthy, able to achieve the potential of your life even after the death of your friend.

THE STAGES OF GRIEVING

Grieving is a continuous process — continuous just as the transition the patient makes from being healthy to facing the end of life is continuous. Grieving generally follows three stages: an initial stage, a middle stage, and a resolution stage. Dividing the process in this way is only intended to make a continuous process easier to talk about. As with bad news, people in grief go backward and forward as emotions come and go in cycles.

The Initial Stage of Grief

The initial phase of grief often seems like shock. Bereaved relatives use words like "numb," "in shock," and "dazed" to describe it. This kind of reaction (which is, again, similar to a patient's reaction to hearing bad news) is partly protective. It's part of the way we assimilate a vast change in our world. We tend to blank out before tackling reality in manageable pieces.

After the shock, a deep sadness often follows. You may find yourself crying when the dead person is mentioned or when her memory crops up. The amount of crying varies tremendously from person to person — there's no "correct" amount. It also varies from culture to culture. Some cultures encourage, or even demand, a lot of crying; others call for a "stiff upper lip." The keys here are the depth of your feeling, and the way you usually express yourself. Vera was a woman in her early seventies whose husband died of a lymphoma. They had been married for nearly fifty years and Vera simply could not stop crying in the early stages of her grief. She said repeatedly that she did not want to live and could see no point in carrying on.

John Martin and I did not ask her to stop crying (that never helps) but we did ask her to not make any decision — including suicide — for at least six months. During that time, she attended the bereavement group at our hospital and came to realize that her crying was "permissible" and, in the circumstances, normal. By being "allowed" to continue crying — although not being "permitted" to commit suicide — she progressed through her grief, and now leads an independent and fulfilling life of her own, something she thought she would never achieve.

So if you normally express your emotions freely, and if you previously cried easily, and if you now feel like crying a lot, then that is what you should do. If you have always been a person who finds public (or private) displays of emotion awkward or embarrassing, then you're not going to change overnight, nor should you.

Some problems are caused by what other people say you should be doing. Quite often, bereaved people are advised by their family and friends to "be strong." What the well-meaning friends are actually saying is: "Please don't cry. It upsets us and we can't really handle it." This is advice, however well meant, that you do not have to take.

Some bereaved people believe they should be strong because that is what the person who has died would have wished. Sometimes the dying person makes that request specifically: "Don't cry — you'll need to be strong afterward." It is important to remember that crying is *not* the opposite of being strong. You can cry *and* be strong. In fact, you can regain strength more quickly if you acknowledge to yourself, by crying, the depth of your hurt. If you *don't* acknowledge that pain and hurt, you probably won't get strong. So try, in this initial phase, to pay attention to the pain you are feeling and to express it as you usually would.

In this initial phase of grieving, you are quite likely to have physical symptoms. You may feel symptoms of anxiety and distress: nausea, pain in the chest or throat, a sensation of difficulty in breathing, general aches and pains, and, for women, menstrual irregularities. Some bereaved persons also develop "sympathetic" symptoms, related to the symptoms experienced by the person who has now died: chest pains if he died of heart disease, or changes in bowel habits if it was cancer of the colon, for example. Developing physical and sympathetic symptoms is quite common, and not a sign that you are losing your health or mind.

The Middle Stage of Grief

The middle stage of grief is the phase during which you begin to realize that life will go on after your bereavement, even though you may not yet see how. It may begin a few weeks after the death, but if you have been through a lot of anticipatory grief, it may begin sooner. During this phase, the shock and the numbing begin to fade away, and life begins to adopt some semblance of normality. In practice, the "semblance of normality" often creates problems in itself. Quite often, your own friends and supporters who may have rallied around and become close and attentive immediately after your bereavement, now see you reassembling your life, and they withdraw and begin to return to their own lives. They assume that you're "going to be fine now."

While you may look all right, you feel anything but. Grieving relatives and spouses have described this phase to me as "hollow," "feeling like a sham," "feeling like a ghost," "not being there." In this state you carry out the actions of a "normal" person, but you're not at all normal inside.

The first thing to realize is that this experience of "not feeling normal" is actually normal *for this stage of your bereavement*. Readjusting to life without the person you've lost is a huge task. It takes time. While you readjust, your emotions and behavior cannot be the same as they were before your loss. Research studies show that the middle phase of grief is often the most difficult. Six months or so after the bereavement, the survivor may well be feeling very low and depressed, while his friends and relatives have come to assume that the worst is over. If you find that this is happening to you, tell your friends how you feel and ask for a bit more support. You may even require professional help from a psychotherapist or grief counselor if things do not improve with time.

Often someone may expect a grieving relative to get over his grief quickly. The following is perhaps the most extreme example I've come across, but it certainly illustrates this difficult problem.

I mentioned Deborah previously. She was "not allowed" to talk about dying by her husband, Harry, who physically obstructed her speech. Harry's father was himself a physician of the "old school," who very rarely expressed any emotions. Deborah's parents were the opposite of Harry's. Deborah's mother was a woman of deep emotions expressed readily and sincerely. Both of Deborah's parents found Deborah's illness almost impossible to bear. They sat with her all day, hardly eating, crying often. The night that Deborah died, her parents were absolutely distraught. I accompanied them while they took their leave of her, and sat with them for some time afterward, while they cried. Harry's father was waiting outside the room. As I came out, about an hour after Deborah's death, I heard him ask Harry, "What are they [Deborah's parents] doing in there — same old performance, eh?"

I was taken aback. Here was a man, himself a physician, who clearly *expected* that parents should be able to get over their grief in less than an hour, and should be able to stop crying before (quite literally) the body was cold. Here was a man clearly incapable of expressing or dealing with his own emotions, who was made visibly uncomfortable by anyone else's. The example of the father certainly explained some of Harry's own problems.

I doubt that many people expect grief to be completed in an hour, but outsiders may be very uncomfortable with your grief, and may wish it to be over so that *their* discomfort is shortened. All you can do, as a grieving person, is be aware of their discomfort, and accept that they aren't going to be much support to you at that time. These things vary as time passes. Someone who is uncomfortable one week may be better able to support you the next week, if you "give them a rest." Furthermore, some people may be able to support you better if you acknowledge their discomfort. You can easily say things such as, "I know that when I talk about how rotten I feel, it makes you uncomfortable. . . ." Sometimes such an understanding sentiment makes things easier all around. It cannot do harm.

Being pushed into returning to normality isn't the only problem at this stage. There are often other processes that are equally wearing on you. You may start questioning aspects of the past, often to do with your friend's illness: What if you had made him go to the doctor earlier? What if you had insisted he try that experimental therapy? What if we hadn't had that argument the week before he died? This kind of question is common, often painful, and generally unsolvable. Of course you cannot simply forget those questions and put them out of your mind. You can't forget them any more than you can forget a toothache or a headache. The questions exist, and they may plague you and occupy your thoughts and even your dreams. These questions are a normal part of the grieving process. You have to accept the fact that most survivors go through the same thing; that most of those questions are simply unanswerable; and that the pain and sadness they cause you will fade as the grief itself resolves.

There is also resentment. As in the early phases of your friend's illness, you may experience very strong feelings of anger and resentment, directed against others who have not lost their spouse, parent, child, or friend as you have, or against healthy people who resemble the person you have lost. After Leslie's death, Ruth found that she felt very strong resentment for many months. She expressed it this way: "Whenever I went out, I would look at every young man and try and decide whether his life was worth more or less than Leslie's. Did this man have children? Was he educated? Would he contribute to the betterment of society as a whole? This kind of question would often lead me on into a silent rant about the absurdity of a God who could destroy a valuable life in its prime."

After a time, for most people, grief will resolve. That resolution is a phase in and of itself.

The Resolution Phase

Not all authorities on grieving agree about the resolution of grief. It is reasonable, however, to suggest that grief has been resolved when the survivor is able to remember the person who has died with fondness and pleasure, to recall the good moments without acute pain and distress, although (perhaps) with some regret. Resolution has something to do with being whole again, and living an independent life — although a life different from that led before the bereavement. While a considerable proportion of people never *completely* resolve their grief, most people do achieve a large measure of resolution.

There are, of course, problems particular to the resolution phase. Some family members and outsiders may feel that, in the resolution phase, you shouldn't be going out with other people (if it is your spouse that has died), having fun, or starting to live a normal life. "It's too soon . . ." or "It's as if he'd never existed" are incredibly painful observations to someone as her grief resolves and she emerges into the real world again.

There's no fixed timetable for resolution. As long as you're moving toward it, it doesn't matter if you achieve it in three months or two years; it's the process that counts. Ruth vividly remembers a remark that revealed other people's attitudes. About two months after Leslie had died several close members of his family came to dinner. Later, one of them, a very well-meaning man, took Ruth aside and said, "Look, you're young and you've got most of your life ahead of you. In four or five years you may meet someone, and I just want you to know that nobody will blame you."

Ruth's reaction was: "Four or five years? What does that mean? Does that mean that if I *don't* appear to be a grieving widow for a full five years, then I didn't love Leslie? Will that be how they measure how much I loved him?"

The whole point is, it's your timetable, not your friends'. You alone know the depth of your feelings and the depth of your grief. However well meant, other people's agendas are not what you need.

Anticipatory Grief

Anticipatory grief is grief that begins before the patient has died. I've mentioned it several times already. Thinking about someone's death before she has died is commonly seen as, in a way, wishing her dead. In Shakespeare's *King Henry IV (Part 2)*, for instance, while the king is dying, his son Prince Hal (Harry) muses about the terrible duties of monarchy that he'll face when his father dies. His father finds that he has taken the crown from his pillow, and, when Harry says that he thought his father had already died, replies: "Thy wish was father, Harry, to that thought."

Though I hate to argue with authorities as great as kings (or Shakespeare), anticipatory grief is not necessarily a thought fathered by a wish to see the person dead. It is, rather, a perfectly normal reaction in preparation for a bereavement. We grieve before a death just as we flinch when we anticipate being injured.

However, anticipatory grief, no matter how natural, does produce some particular problems. If the patient *doesn't* die, or doesn't die within the anticipated time, then the relative who has been going through anticipatory grief tends to feel two emotions: first, a sense of guilt for having "mentally buried" the still-living patient; and second, a tendency to blame the patient for having put friends and family through a false bereavement. This actually happened in my own case, leaving my wife and me as virtual strangers at the time of my recovery. To put it simply, anticipatory grief should not make you feel guilty. Try to accept it as natural. Do remember, however, that the final phase of illness can be quite prolonged and that you may end up feeling impatient, and then guilty. You can't necessarily prevent these feelings, but being aware of them is helpful.

WHEN GRIEF GOES WRONG

Thus far, I have only dealt with the way in which normal grief does its work and allows the survivor to reshape her life and reinvest her emotions in new relationships. But for some people, grief doesn't work out. They get stuck in the middle of grieving. Grief that goes wrong and doesn't complete the healing is called "pathological grief." It can be quite a problem.

One young woman had very clear problems with arrested grief. Donna was only twelve when her father died suddenly and unexpectedly. Her mother was deeply shocked, and would not allow anyone in the family to talk about him or to cry openly. Instead, she concentrated very hard on getting the whole family, including Donna, back to "normal." Donna carried on with her schooling and went on to college. She got a job as a personal assistant to an important politician. But lots of little things began to go wrong: she had headaches, lost concentration, developed memory problems, broke into fits of crying, and had difficulties with her boyfriends.

She was referred to an excellent psychotherapist. He helped her understand that, because of her mother's well-meaning efforts, she'd never gone through the whole process of grief. So — twelve years after the event — Donna went through the process of mourning her father, this time with the therapist. The effects were quite dramatic. Within a few weeks, Donna was in top form emotionally, professionally, and personally.

Perhaps the most crucial message to take from Donna's experience is "It's never too late." Even twelve years after the event, with the right supervision, grieving can achieve a great deal.

So how can you tell whether you are experiencing a slow process of normal grief or if you're stuck and experiencing pathological grief? Look for certain signs in yourself, and see if you are changing over a period of time. Think about the pain you feel when you remember the person who has died, the feelings you have when his name is mentioned unexpectedly, when you meet someone with the same name, or when you visit a place that was special for the two of you. Think about how you're making out with new relationships and friendships. Think about how much time you spend crying, and how well you sleep at night. Think about how often you recall and relive the last moments of your friend's life.

And then try to understand whether the pain is decreasing. Not day by day or week by week, but over a period of months. Are things better today than they were six months ago? (Note that I'm not saying "Have you got over all your grief in six months?" What I'm asking is "Are you making progress that you can measure in six months?" There's a very important difference.)

If you're not making progress at all and everything that hurt six months ago still hurts with the same intensity, and if you are continuously reliving the last few days of your friend's life, you are stuck, and you should seek professional help, specifically psychotherapy. You might wish to try a self-help group first if you're feeling especially nervous. Most bereavement groups (if arranged by experienced people) are good at detecting pathological grief; if they can't help you move forward, they will encourage you to seek help and will give you the courage to ask for it.

Another sign of incomplete grieving is a failure to move on, a failure to grow. I've often seen stunted emotional growth in widows of dominating husbands. These widows live by the same rules their husbands set while still alive, as if life in 1988 had to be lived according to the person who died in 1968, for example, and not by the person who survives him. If you find yourself living in a big house "because Dad would have wanted it that way," or taking on some burden that you'd rather be without because you feel it would be disloyal to do otherwise, think again. And if you find that your day-to-day life is ruled by ghosts and not by you, then try to get some help. Grieving properly means being able to live your own life after bereavement, not reenacting a daily imitation of what went before.

9

Spiritual Aspects

Religious beliefs are intensely personal and vary from person to person. Some people have a definite, personal image of God, others having a strong but imprecise sensation. Many, on the other hand, don't know whether there is a God, or are certain that there isn't one. Strong religious beliefs can inspire the patient and those around him. A professor in our medical school had such a firm belief in life after death that he underwent the final phase of his illness with total and unshakable equanimity. He spoke of his imminent death as one might speak of a summer holiday. The extent of the support he gained from his belief impressed those who looked after him, even though some of us felt a little uncomfortable at first.

These personal beliefs are often even more central to the patient's world view than politics, food, music, or even sex. Many people may go through most of their life without discussing their religious feelings with friends or family who are otherwise fairly close. Discussing religious views may be a delicate matter at any time. It is particularly delicate as the patient faces death — an event that challenges religious beliefs almost more than any other.

So many books have been written on the subject of man's relationship to God or his images of God, and so much of that writing is concerned with the mystery of death, that it might seem invidious to summarize the subject here. It is, however, important to consider the pragmatic and practical issues raised by religious beliefs that drastically affect the care of a dying patient. What I call "good" religion, a firm and consistent religious belief that sustains and supports the patient, that does not attack the religious views of the family or friends, needs no comment, precisely because it works well for the patient and family. However, it sometimes happens that religion becomes a stumbling block, either for the patient himself, or for the relationship between the patient and family. It is in these circumstances that outside perspective can be useful.

I shall concentrate particularly on two relatively familiar situations: one in which there has been some element of "bad" theology, and the other in which there are major religious differences between patient and supporters. However, in order to demonstrate some ways of approaching these problems, I have to address two other theological issues. The first is the most commonly asked theological question: "Dear God, why me?" The second is the therapeutic value and the meaning of prayer to the patient, as seen by the friend and supporter.

In preparing this chapter, I have discussed the major issues with several ministers and particularly with John Martin, drawing on his experience as a hospital chaplain, in which capacity he has supported many of my patients. John and I have markedly different religious beliefs. The fact that we work so closely together demonstrates that it is not necessary to have the same religious views as other people in order to understand them and talk freely with them — a point that I hope is underlined in this chapter.

"Dear God, Why Me?"

In earlier chapters I pointed out that "Why me?" is often not a question as such, but a cry of distress, a plea for help, an expression of guilt, or a mixture of these and other emotions. The difference between "Why me?" and "Dear God, why me?" is that the second of these is directed specifically at God, and at that particular person's personal image of God. That question may contain all the anger, rage, despair, and frustration that is contained in the secular "Why me?" but it also addresses questions of faith.

These questions of faith contain three major elements. First, there is a sense of rage against God for allowing this illness to happen. Second, there may be a strong sense of disappointment. The patient may feel that she has faithfully observed her personal religion all her life, and is now being abandoned and cheated of the reward she expected. Third, there may be guilt, borne of a sense that God has inflicted this illness as a punishment for wrongdoing in the past.

Each aspect of the question will cause distress if it is assumed that the God in whom the patient believes is the prime mover of the person's life, the God who controls all that happens to that person. Many ministers do not accept this older image of God. They do not accept that God is some sort of divine puppeteer who can intervene on the patient's behalf if He wants to. Many, particularly those who work with dying patients, believe that the essence of the relationship between a person and God is the way in which God works with the person, in the face of vicissitudes and setbacks that are a fact of life. In this view of religion, the illness and threat of death are not due to dereliction, abandonment, or punishment on the part of God, but are instead part of the process of life. Even though these events seem inevitable, it is *permissible* and even *healthy* to question God. Furthermore, many ministers uphold the view that asking "Dear God, why me?" is a way of bringing the person closer to a personal understanding of his own faith.

Ralph, a personnel manager in his late sixties, a deeply religious Christian all his life, found himself questioning his faith near the end. He felt a strong sense of disappointment and abandonment. He didn't feel that his illness was a punishment, nor was he angry; but he was in great distress because he thought that God had let him down. This feeling made him sense that his personal faith was inadequate, and he blamed himself for not having a strong enough belief to see him through the bad times.

I asked John Martin to see him. John made the following points: "In the Jewish and Christian faiths, believers accept the fact that people were created free in God's image. They accept that, as free beings, they are not controlled by some sort of divine controller, but rather that they make their own decisions. To suggest that God moves us on a board like some chess player moving his pieces is ridiculous. It goes against all good theology that I know. To suggest that God is with us as we struggle in life, that God is part of us as we experience our aches and pains, our joys and our celebrations is good theology and makes perfect sense. The need to blame God for our pain, our loss, our hurt isn't unusual, nor is it nonsensical. The fact of the matter is that good theology would suggest that God is not at the root of all evil, illness, pain, and suffering, but that He works with us to combat those things as part of us. Pain and suffering always have been. Unfortunately, they always will be, as well."

For Ralph, reconciliation with his faith was not difficult. He accepted that his faith was part of his struggle, not a means to overcome his physical illness. He came to understand that his illness was not a failure of faith or of his own personal resources.

In making the important point that God is not the *cause* of pain and suffering, but that He works with us to combat those things as part of us, John is able to speak with the authority of a church minister backed up by much theological writing. The pedigree of this view of religion adds to the support it can give a patient going through a crisis of faith. From a theological viewpoint, many accept the view that it is permissible and healthy for people to question their faith. The feelings of disappointment, rage, and guilt expressed in the phrase "Dear God, why me?" are neither rare nor abnormal.

The Function of Prayer

As someone trained in the scientific method and lacking strong religious convictions, it may seem out of place for me to assess the value of prayer. After all, prayer is not scientific or medical; it is spiritual, mystical, and intimate. It is, in essence, the spiritual relationship between the one who is praying and God at work. But while personal and subjective, it still produces an observable effect. Whether or not one has the same religious belief as the patient, it is still possible to see the effect of prayer and to comment on it, in the same way that one can observe the effect of counseling, painkillers, or antidepressants.

What is clear, even to the outsider, about the mental and spiritual activity we call prayer is that it is a transaction between the person who prays and her God. Usually, the action of prayer in itself brings relief: the activity of putting into words a description of the current state of things, of emotions, physical sufferings, hopes, and disappointments is in itself therapeutic. John Martin describes it as "an appropriate response, a real response to whatever is happening to us at a given point in our lives. If God is our Guide, our Friend, our Helper, then we need to be able to have an open and honest relationship with Him. That relationship can be very helpful and very therapeutic for the person with the illness. It can be one that allows us freedom of expression and freedom of feeling. If life is good, it needs to be celebrated, it needs to be expressed and embraced. If life is not so good, then, that too needs to be recognized in some response to a God that we keep nothing from, a God that we can share with all levels, painful and positive, helpful and harmful, good and bad.

"The prayer relationship between the believer and his God can be very therapeutic. It can be the only way for some people to unload, to express themselves, to get rid of their feelings. Some people are unable to share on that level with another human being, and for them especially that sharing, that relationship with their God becomes very meaningful. Even those people who have a good rapport and good communication with those around them may be unable to reach the same sort of intimate or close level with another human being that they feel they can reach with their God. No one, a believer will tell you, knows them as well, as deeply, as closely and as personally as their God. This is a time to capitalize on that relationship, to make use of it, to draw help, strength, courage, wholeness and health from it."

This is a point often missed by those of us who don't pray: prayer is a response to what is going on in life, and, as such, acts as a therapeutic help to the person who prays. But many prayers contain requests or pleas for help, a cure, a miracle, relief. What happens if these requests are not granted, if the disease or the symptoms don't improve? In other words, what happens if it seems that prayers are not being answered? John, like most hospital chaplains, has encountered that question almost every day, and feels that many prayers are requests for miracles. But, he says: "We know that God is not in the habit of snapping His fingers and making things change. As a matter of fact, that is a very foreign picture of the God that we know and experience in our day-to-day life. But all things can be brought to God: our concerns, our fears, and our joys. Just as a child would go to a parent with a hurt or a pain, the believer needs to be able to go to God, because in the relationship, in the expression of the pain, the hurt or the need, lies the therapeutic ability of the spiritual expression to give ease and to alleviate suffering. A child knows that the parent can't make the scrape on her knee go away but, in going to the parent and in telling the parent what hurts and in seeking the parent, the child gets comfort in being close to the parent. The act of seeking makes the relationship closer."

Again, this is a point that is very often overlooked. The act of making a request draws the person nearer, whether or not the request is answered, and whether or not it is *expected* to be answered.

Thus far we have been dealing with the positive aspects of religious belief that you, the friend, can encourage and welcome. Let us now move on to more difficult areas, where religion may present obstacles and cause suffering rather than relieve it.

"Bad" Theology

"Bad" theology can best be defined as theology that is oppressive, manipulative, destructive, and narrow. It is almost always based entirely on concepts of reward and punishment.

I can best illustrate the effects of bad theology by describing the care of Angela, in her early forties when I first met her. She had advanced breast cancer which had spread to the lungs, causing breathing difficulty. The cancer had initially responded to chemotherapy, but after several months it worsened again and was resistant to drugs. She became deeply depressed and virtually uncommunicative. After a couple of weeks, the depression grew so severe that we asked the opinion of a psychiatrist, and Angela was admitted to the hospital to start antidepressant therapy. She improved a little and was discharged from the hospital, but I was constantly struck by how great her depression was compared to her noticeable, but not severe, physical disabilities. After a few outpatient appointments, I got to know her and her husband, Richard, a little better, and managed to ask her whether she had any thoughts about dying. She cried very hard. When I asked her what was her greatest fear about dying, she said she was unable to tell me. When I asked whether she would like to speak to our hospital chaplain, she said she would.

Her breathing had worsened again and she now required continuous oxygen. She got into a terrible panic if the mask was removed even for a few seconds, so she came into the hospital again.

John Martin got to know Angela and Richard well. He noted that Angela was more petrified of her illness and her upcoming death than anyone he had ever seen before. After they had spent a long while together, she confided in John that for some time she had been a member of a strong fundamentalist church movement, that had originated in the United States. Shortly after her original diagnosis of breast cancer she had been told by members of this church that if she went to their church regularly and prayed seriously, God would free her from her illness if He was interested in saving her. If, on the other hand, God did not cure her, then this was His will, and it was His way of punishing her on earth, and preparing her for even greater punishment after death. As her physical condition deteriorated, she was told that what she was going through was nothing compared to what would happen after death. This was all part of God's punishment for the success she and her husband shared on earth, and for having a comfortable life-style and home. Her husband, Richard, was not a member of that church. He was very distressed by what Angela had been told, but he had promised not to tell anyone else about her beliefs. She had begged him not to, for fear it might make her punishment worse still. Her children had also heard much of their mother's beliefs. The older child was very skeptical about Hell and punishment, but the younger son, Robert, was very worried.

John spent a lot of time undoing the harm, and I was able to see the effects of what he said to the family, and to reinforce them. Her breathing symptoms were so bad because she was afraid that each attack of breathlessness was signaling the end of her life, and the start of her punishment in Hell. As John removed the threats of dire punishment, her symptoms improved noticeably. She spent time out of bed without oxygen, she was then able to walk without it, and eventually she could even go to the smoking lounge and have a cigarette (something I would never encourage in other circumstances!). She began to smile more, and to laugh, and she became closer to Richard (who was also very relieved at what was happening) and to her family. We were able to discuss the end of her life with greater calm. Together we all decided that a palliative care unit would be the most suitable place. She died, peacefully, a few weeks later.

I think Angela's story is important because it shows that the effect of bad theology can be so subtle and yet so powerful. Quite often, patients threatened in this way have been told not to talk about their fears to other people, so finding out the truth can be quite tricky. However, if you can spend the time listening, you may find clues as to what is being held back from you. You probably will not be able to undo the effects of bad theology by yourself; it almost always requires someone with authority within a church or other religious organization.

Differences in Belief

Differences in religious belief may sometimes appear to be so fundamental and so divisive that any form of communication can be threatened. (The history of so-called holy wars from the Crusades to the Troubles in modern-day Ireland are reminders of the power of these forces.) But, when we pause for a moment to remind ourselves and each other of what we are trying to do, the differences can fade into the background.

With so many different religions in existence, it must be obvious that no single religion has a monopoly on truth, morality, or all the answers to life's questions. So when a person is facing the end of her life, we as friends should be looking at the practical value of that person's religion in her life. It is a complete waste of our time and energy to worry about whether or not our friend's religion is the true path to eternal truth. Provided that the patient is not laboring under some manipulative and destructive theological guilt, all that we need to do is to help our friend use her own religion to help herself. To borrow a well-worn phrase, our attitude should simply be "if it works for you, do it."

Looking after many dying patients, I have met believers in the majority of the world's religions. I have never encountered a problem so severe that it halted communication. Working closely with professionals who are members of various different religions I have often called upon their various expert skills for help with patients. You can do the same. As long as you make the effort to understand as much as you can about your friend's religious beliefs, and as long as you try to see how those beliefs help him, then the fact that he holds a different set of beliefs shouldn't be a problem. Your main goal should be to understand and respect his choice.

WHAT YOU CAN DO

In summary, to support the patient in her spiritual understanding of death, keep the following in mind:

1. *Decide if You Are Close Enough to Approach the Topic.* A person's feelings about her religious beliefs are among her most intimate. You probably should not open a discussion with the patient about them unless you are quite close. Try to gauge how close a friend you are, and what level of intimacy you share.

2. *Be Sensitive.* Tread delicately.

3. *Try to Decide if Bad Theology Is Doing Harm.* This also requires sensitivity and a readiness to listen without leaping to premature judgment or condemnation. If you cannot decide whether or not the patient is being supported by his religious beliefs, then . . .

4. *Get Help.* You may find a discussion with a chaplain, social worker, or psychotherapist helpful. Remember that if you're talking about the patient specifically, you should get the patient's consent to have the conversation. If you just want general guidelines about good and bad theology, you should feel free to talk to anyone.

5. *Honor the Patient's Choice.* This is no time to try to convert someone to your view of the world. If her religious beliefs happen to differ from yours, honor and support them *as long as they work for the patient.*

6. *Don't Be Afraid to Talk about It if the Patient Wants To.* Just as it is helpful to allow the patient to talk about sexual problems, however awkward or embarrassing, you can help the patient by being there and listening when he wants to talk about his personal religious beliefs.

III
PRACTICALITIES

10

Things Every Caregiver Should Do

One of the most common problems for friends and relatives trying to help a dying person is that they simply don't know where to start. They want to help, but don't know what to do first. In the preceding chapters, I have discussed several approaches to the problems that your friend may encounter. In this chapter I am going to set out a logical trail for you to follow, one which will help you decide where your help is most useful and where you can start. In Chapter 11, I shall go on to offer guidelines that deal with your specific relationship to the dying person, but the outline in this chapter is a basic guide applicable to anybody who wants to help.

CHECKLIST FOR OFFERING HELP

1. *Make Your Offer.* You must first find out whether or not your help is wanted. If there are other people involved in support, you should find out whether your help is needed. If it is, make your offer. Your initial offer should

be specific, not just, "let me know if there's anything I can do." Say clearly that you'll check back to see if there are things you can help with. Obviously, if you are the parent of a sick child or the spouse of a patient, you don't need to ask; but in most other circumstances it is important to know whether you can be in the right position to help. Sometimes a distant acquaintance or colleague is *more* welcome than a close relative, so don't prejudge your usefulness. Do not be upset if the patient does not seem to want your support. Do not take it personally. If the patient cannot use your help, see if there are other family members who need assistance. After you have made your initial offer, do not wait to be called, but check back with a few preliminary suggestions.

2. *Become Informed.* If you are to be useful to your friend, you will need some information about what the medical situation is, but only enough to make sensible plans. You do not need to, nor should you, become a world expert on the subject. Many helpers are drawn to acquire more and more details, details not necessarily relevant to their friend's situation. Sometimes their motive is curiosity, while sometimes it reflects a desire to be in control.

3. *Assess the Needs.* This means assessing the needs of the patient and of the rest of the family. Naturally, any assessment is going to be full of uncertainties because the future is often unpredictable, but try to think carefully about the patient's needs. Who is going to look after him during the day? Can he get from bed to toilet? Can he prepare his own meals? Does he need medications that he cannot take himself? And of the other family members: are there children that need to be taken to and from school? Is

the spouse medically fit, or are there things she needs? Is the home suitable for the patient's medical condition or are there things that need to be done there? Start your list by going through a day in the life of your friend, deciding what he will need at each stage.

4. *Decide What You Can Do and Want to Do.* What are you good at? Can you cook for the patient? (Even taking around precooked frozen meals is always welcome.) Can you prepare meals for other family members? Are you handy around the house? Could you put up handrails or wheelchair ramps if required? Could you house-sit, so that the spouse can visit the patient? Could you take the kids out to the zoo for the day to give the couple some time together? If you aren't good at any of these things, would you be prepared to pay for, say, a cleaner for a half day a week to help out? Could you get hold of relevant booklets for the patient? Can you find videos that the patient likes? Does the patient need the furniture rearranged? (For instance, the patient may need to sleep on the ground floor because she cannot manage stairs.) If so, could you help her do it? Will there be flowers at home when the patient gets out of the hospital?

5. *Start Out with Small, Practical Things.* Look at the list of the things you can do and are prepared to do, and start off by offering a few of them. Do not offer all of them — this will overwhelm the patient. Pick some small, practical items that the patient *might not be able to do for herself easily*. Making a small contract and meeting your target is far better than aiming too high and failing. A little extra thought may find you some "inside knowledge." For instance, one patient, David, used to get his hair cut every week. It was a small but significant part of his regular

routine. When David was in the hospital, his friend Joseph arranged for the hospital barber to call weekly. There are lots of similarly thoughtful touches, like mowing the patient's lawn when he's unable to, preparing meals, or house-sitting. Another patient, Dora, was a schoolteacher, and her colleagues at the school got the children to draw cards for her. Again, these thoughtful little tasks were highly valued by the patients.

6. *Avoid Excesses.* Huge gifts can overwhelm and embarrass. Don't buy the patient a new car, for instance, unless you know specifically that this is wanted, that you can comfortably afford such an expense, and that it will not cause embarrassment. Most large gifts spring from a sense of guilt on the part of the donor, and create guilt in the recipient. Similarly, your offers of help should be modest and suited to the patient and family. Be sensitive with your generosity.

7. *Listen.* Time is a present you can always give. Chapter Two provided some guidelines on sensitive listening. Spend regular time with your friend. If you can only spend two hours once a month, that's fine. But ten or fifteen minutes every day or two establishes a much-welcomed sense of continuity. Be reliable and be there for the patient.

8. *Involve Other People.* Be fair to yourself and recognize your own limitations. Every helper and supporter wants to do his or her best, and you may be very tempted to undertake heroic tasks, out of a sense of anger and rage against the injustice of your friend's situation. But if you make heroic gestures and then fail you will become part of the problem, rather than part of the solution. You owe it to yourself and to your friend to undertake reasonable tasks

you can accomplish. You should always be realistic about what you can do, and about getting other people to help with what you can't provide.

Going through this list is valuable because it offers a genuinely practical approach to something that is probably unfamiliar to you, and because it quells your own sense of panic. It gives you a place to start. Whatever plans you make will certainly change with time. Be prepared to be flexible and learn on the job.

11

Individual Relationships

LOSING A PARENT

Some people have called the death of a parent whose children are adult the least unfair of deaths. It is, after all, in the natural order of things that the older generation should die before their children. Yet, for most people, the death of a parent is a huge and painful loss and all that much more painful for being underrated by society at large.

Most parents are the roof over their children's lives. Whether good or bad they have always been there. As their death approaches, we realize that there will be a time when they are no longer there for us. Their influence colors our view of the world so pervasively that we can hardly estimate how important their presence is until we face the reality of their death, and the prospect of life without them. A few years ago, I was talking to a writer about my experience of facing what many thought would be the end of my life. The writer said, "You seemed to take it pretty well. Do you think you would have felt the same if neither of your parents had been alive?" Nobody had ever asked me that before, and I had to admit that much of my own attitude to the illness, my sense that "It's not my turn yet" was based on the fact that both my parents are alive and well. We feel more vulnerable when we lose our parents. We are then the oldest generation; it is our turn next.

So one major cause of the pain of losing a parent (even though it may sound selfish) is the feeling of vulnerability that accompanies the loss of our psychological roof. That vulnerability has little to do with one's sense of dependence or independence. The practical changes in life-style may be worse or more obvious for a child who depended heavily on his parents in adult life. Yet even the most independent child will experience that psychological sense of vulnerability. This vulnerability may be difficult for others to understand. You may get short shrift from your friends ("Come on, your mother is nearly eighty"). You need to be aware that this sense of vulnerability is real and not a sign of extreme weakness or dependence. It is a normal reaction.

A second major cause of pain is the change in your role as your parents near death. Once, they supported you; now you have to support them. This often causes a sense of awkwardness. Even if you have capably cared for other dependents, including friends or your own children, it's often difficult to do the same for your parent. The role reversal may be vivid for both you and your parent, and you may be acutely aware of the fact that you are performing an unfamiliar role with a very familiar person.

Furthermore, depending on the physical problems your parent may suffer, you may have to perform duties that embarrass you both. You might *want* to do these things for your parent, and he might be very grateful for your help, but there will often be embarrassment. Gerald described what it was like when, in his fifties, he found himself emptying a bedpan for his bedridden mother. He said, "At first I thought the embarrassment would overcome both of us. But I said to myself 'It has to be done: and she's done enough for me,' and then I found that I wasn't actually embarrassed at all, but glad to be doing something. And because I wasn't embarrassed, she wasn't either."

To some extent the experience of parental loss differs for sons and daughters. Generalizations are difficult, but daughters often have closer bonds with their mothers, and usually suffer a broader and deeper sense of loss when their mother dies. This may be because many daughters maintain very close contact with their mother, taking them as role models. The loss of a parent, friend, and role model at one blow can be very severe. Sons may experience some of the same losses at the death of their father, but the impact is often less. This is partly because fathers usually have less to do with raising the children, and partly because fathers often instill a sense of independence at an early age into their sons, thereby reducing the intimacy of their later relationship.

However, general rules are not that important. What matters is the closeness and the intimacy that you experience with your mother or father, and how you can help and support them in the best way possible. What follows is a guide to working out your parent's needs, and discovering how you can try to meet them. Working through a schedule of decisions like this won't solve all your problems, and it certainly won't stop the pain, but it may help you get a grip on what's happening, so that events will not overrun you completely.

A GUIDE TO MAKING PLANS

1. *Get Informed — But Don't Become a World Expert.* Find out what disease or condition your mother or father has, and find out — in broad outline — what effect it's likely to have. You probably won't help your parent by reading every textbook and medical journal on the subject. Children who do that are often working out of a sense of guilt or a desire to take command of their parent's life. That may not be what the patient wants at all. You need to be informed enough to prepare for what's ahead. It's certainly worth contacting the local self-help groups and information services (for example, cancer societies, Alzheimer's groups, and motoneuron disease groups) and reading booklets on the disease, but if you find yourself spending hours in the medical library you should ask yourself whom you're doing that for and whom it's meant to help.

2. *Try to Get a Picture of What Lies Ahead.* This will almost always be vague and uncertain. The doctor looking after your parent will only be able to help a bit, because all diseases are variable, many immensely so. Even rapidly progressive diseases may end someone's life in from three months to a year, for instance, a time span that is large enough to make planning difficult. While you have to accept uncertainty, however frustrating and painful, you should try to get some idea of the range of future scenarios. For example, in one case, the patient might be fine for many months and then quickly decline, or she might get worse slowly and steadily. The true picture may only emerge with time. You may have to wait several months before your parent's doctor can get a more accurate impression of the disease's progress. That's hard on all of you, but it's a fact.

3. *Assemble a List of Possible Needs*. Based on what information you have, try to estimate your parent's possible needs, in both physical and social terms. Will he be able to cook for himself? Who will do the house cleaning? Is he able to get in and out of the bath or onto and off the toilet? Is he able to call you if he needs help? Can he remember phone numbers and manage the phone? Can he manage stairs? If not, can a bed be made on the ground floor? There are dozens of similar questions. You can create a thorough list by mentally following a whole day in your parent's life. Imagine his day from morning to bedtime. At each stage try to imagine what he will need in order to manage. While your list may not be immediately accurate, at least you will be able to make a start. His needs will become clearer as time goes on.

4. *Try to Find Out What Your Parent Wants*. You should not rush this part of your planning. Nobody coping with the impact of a serious disease can make all future plans at once. But over a period of time, you should try to find out if your parent has strong feelings about decisions such as whether she wants to be looked after at home, and whether she would like to move in with you or any other relative. Your parent may have a very clear idea of what she wants, or it may take time for the picture to emerge. It's important to find out her wishes. Raise the various options and see how your parent feels. What about nursing homes? Palliative care units and hospices? What are her thoughts about trying to stay at home with visiting nurses and a homemaker service? Can you help by getting more information — for instance by visiting a local nursing home or hospice and reporting back? Can you get more information from the local social services? If you simply go ahead and make plans that you think are appropriate you

run the risk of offending and insulting your parent — as happened to my friend Robert. He and his brother Michael arranged a move to a nursing home for their mother without consulting her, resulting in the family equivalent of a civil war lasting for several weeks. They were eventually reconciled, once their mother had made them realize that she still had opinions on the subject of her own fate. But those few weeks were most unhappy for all of them.

5. *Make a List of Your Resources*. This means making a list of the resources available both to your parent and to you. Is your other parent still alive? If so, how much is he able to do for the ill parent? Who is responsible for what in your parents' household at present?

Then think about what you have available. How much time and effort can you personally devote to your parent's care this week or month? And, if the patient's condition deteriorates over many months, how much time can you devote then? Be realistic, and resist the temptation to be a hero in the initial planning stage. You will feel worse if you don't meet your goals later.

Try to obtain information about outside resources, especially social services such as homemaker services, meals on wheels, aids to daily living (handrails in the bathroom and wheelchair ramps, for instance), and domestic cleaning services, to cite a few examples.

6. *Start by Making "What If . . ." Plans*. Rather than mapping the whole future at once, take it in bite-sized chunks. Start by working out what you can do if your parent's condition stays approximately the same for a time. Who will do what? Try to match the needs you've thought about with what your parent wants, and what you have available. If you have a family of your own, don't make these decisions alone. One of the worst things you

can do is to commit family resources without first consulting your family. "You'll come and live with us, Mother — won't she, Joe?" is an invitation to disaster. It creates serious guilt in both your family and your parent, and puts you in the center of a potentially damaging conflict.

7. *Take It One Step at a Time, and Be Realistic.* It's better to make small contracts with your parent and meet them reliably than to try to take over all his care and then fail. He will feel abandoned if you don't do what you promised, and you will end up feeling guilty. Make realistic plans and stick to them. Remember also that as time goes on, the routines of caring for the terminally ill become a burden, and the glamour of volunteering to do everything fades quickly.

8. *Accept That All Plans Should Be Flexible and May Change.* This applies to every plan and at every stage. Your parent may be very excited to live at home when she is discharged from the hospital, but when she tries it, even with full social services, it doesn't work and she feels miserable. Or she may have decided, at a later stage, to be admitted to a hospice or palliative care unit, only to dislike it when she arrives (although that's rare in practice). You have to be flexible. If you find your plans are changing, it's probably because the situation is changing. It doesn't mean you made the wrong decisions at the start.

LISTENING AND TALKING

A child's relationship with his parent can be as varied as anything in the human species. It can be close and loving; or it may be a continued cat-and-dog struggle which actually contains a great deal of love, intimacy, and dependence (as perfectly illustrated in the film *Terms of*

Endearment); and it may be genuinely distant and remote, or even deeply antagonistic. Whatever the relationship, as a child becomes an adult he develops independence, and the nature of his reliance on his parents alters. Robin Skynner, an expert family therapist, suggests, in his book *Families — And How to Survive Them,* that the final stage of growing up into independence is achieved when you can be friends with your parents. That means putting aside the conflicts that developed as you were gaining your independence, and instead accepting your parents as they are.

That may not be easy. If, for example, you have a strong feeling that your parents have never acknowledged your true worth, and have been unappreciative of your talents and support, then you may feel resentful if you now have to look after them. Accepting them as they are means that you have to try to stop expecting them to change. You have to accept that they are unappreciative and that this is *their* problem, not yours. If, after many years, you feel that your mother is short-tempered and autocratic, then accepting her means accepting her short-tempered and autocratic behavior. You ask yourself, "How can I can help this short-tempered autocratic and ill woman?" not, "How can I change my behavior so that this ill woman will finally appreciate my true worth?"

An example of this that I have never forgotten occurred when I was looking after Dorothy, a woman in her late sixties with very advanced emphysema. She was a most demanding patient. She constantly changed her plans. Her daughter, Anthea, was an attractive, intelligent, and articulate woman who constantly argued with the nurses and medical staff (including me) about her mother's care and needs. After three or four rather difficult exchanges, I arranged an interview with Anthea alone. I told her that while her mother's medical condition was serious she was

not going to die in the next few months, and that we
therefore needed to work together to make plans for her
long-term care. I told Anthea that I found her mother
demanding and manipulative, and I illustrated my point
with a few examples. I said, plainly, "I can't save your
mother's life, because I can't change her or her lungs, but
you can save *your* life if you stop hoping that she will
change." Anthea's face changed instantly. She understood
that other people could see that she was a supportive and
capable woman, even though her mother was constantly
criticizing her. She also realized that her mother was
working her like a puppet, and that this was what was
exhausting her and making her angry. From that moment on, Anthea's response was different. Her mother
still grumbled, but Anthea was neither crushed by the
grumbles nor prodded into having a fight with the nurses
and doctors.

Of course, if you are genuinely and deeply close to your
parents, none of this conflict will be necessary, but for
those who are distant or who have been emotionally separate from their parents for some time, acceptance is very
important. There is no shortcut to acceptance, but listening and talking are the means by which you become closer
if you have been separated. The key to being supportive —
particularly if you have been distant in the past — is to try
to understand and identify your parent's emotion, rather
than simply reacting to the words or actions that express
it. You may have to change the way you react to your
parent, and break the habit of a lifetime. But losing your
parent is a big change that calls for new responses. Think,
for instance, about what might happen if, some time after
receiving the diagnosis, your mother or father says, "I'm
going to die — and I'm just not ready." You may never
before have had to deal with this kind of resentment or

sadness from your mother or father, and you therefore may have little to guide you on how to respond. But, using the principles I have outlined in Chapter 2, Sensitive Listening, you might consider some of these options:

The patient says something like:

"I'm going to die — and I'm not ready."

You have several choices:

You can say:

"Well, you're seventy-five and you've had a rich life."

— may be true but does not respond to the statement.

or

"There is a season for all things."

— dismisses the patient's feelings at that moment.

or

"Don't talk like that."

— shuts the door on any conversation about feelings.

Or you can say:

"It's not easy for you, is it?"

or

"What's the most scary part?"

or

Nothing, just hold your parent's hand.

These responses are all attempts to stay close to the patient and encourage her to talk.

In summary, then, the impending loss of a parent will often have a larger emotional impact than you — or your acquaintances — may expect. It may also carry considerable practical implications for your own life, in that someone who has supported you in the past now requires you to support him. By following the guidelines I have suggested here, you can make some logical and practical inroads.

LOSING A SPOUSE

Losing a spouse may mean losing a person you've lived with most of your life, a partner, friend, lover, supporter, and co-parent. Every marriage or relationship has a different mix of these ingredients. The way a terminal illness affects a marriage varies to a vast extent.

The impact depends primarily on the kind of relationship the partners enjoyed before the illness: their degree of dependence on each other, the depth of their intimacy, the way they share their feelings, and the way each understands the role of the other. The effect of the illness also depends on the age of the partners, their individual attitudes to death and illness, the length of the marriage, and whether or not they have confronted other major problems before. In general, the marriages that best weather the storm are those in which each person has a good understanding of the other's feelings and the other's role in the marriage, and in which both are used to talking about their feelings and resolving the issues that come between them.

Now, you can't create a new relationship in the face of a major threat, but you can take steps to counteract the way the illness tends to separate you. The key is to try to be sensitive to the way your partner is feeling and, at the same time, to be aware of your own feelings. If you can recognize what is happening to each of you, you can lessen the separation that many serious illnesses produce.

During the grind of the illness, the main burden of care will probably fall to you: you become the primary caregiver, the gatekeeper and monitor of other friends and family. This can be grueling and exhausting. While you want to do everything, it's important to let other people help.

You will often feel angry, resentful, or frustrated. The fact that you love your spouse doesn't stop those feelings; in fact, it makes them more likely. And yet, during this time of maximum stress, you are "supposed" to be totally patient and understanding, infinitely tolerant, and endlessly forbearing. Very few people are actually like that. How frightening for the sick person if a spouse suddenly turns into a saint! That is not what supporting a dying person is about. You are not supposed to lose your human reactions and suddenly become a perfect nurse treating your fragile spouse. What you can do is listen more carefully than usual, be aware of her feelings, and give her a bit more leeway, a bit more benefit of the doubt when your feelings or needs conflict.

You strike a balance. On the one hand, try to avoid full-blooded family arguments spurred on by your reactions to the illness. On the other hand, you needn't turn into a Florence Nightingale. That balance isn't easy to strike, but it can be done if you behave *like yourself* while trying to emphasize the kinder and more sensitive parts of yourself (rather than imitating the saintly behavior of someone else).

A GUIDE TO MAKING PLANS

1. *Become Informed — But Don't Become a World Expert.* It is impossible to stress this point too often. You need enough detailed information to make plans for you and your spouse. Neither of you should — or needs to — become a surrogate doctor. If you are spending hours read-

ing medical literature, you are using time that could probably be better spent with your partner.

2. *Think about Your Relationship to Date.* Think about how the two of you have lived with each other in the past. In particular, how clearly defined have your jobs and responsibilities been within the relationship? Has one of you always taken over one area of responsibility, or have you shared everything? Has one of you generally been the "stronger" partner, onto whom the other unloads problems? Or have you taken it in turns, each supporting the other when the need arose? How have you coped with previous problems: illnesses in the family, job changes, financial problems? Who usually makes the plans — or do you usually make them together? If you have children, who has done most of the upbringing? By thinking like this you can work out what is going to be needed as your partner becomes sicker, and how accustomed you will be to shouldering the whole burden.

3. *Try to Estimate Your Future Needs.* This may require much detailed consideration. Predicting the progress of the illness is such an uncertain task. Even so, examine practical things around the house (mobility, access to toilets, ability to manage stairs), and aspects of the medical condition, such as how medicines can be given regularly (particularly if injections or other special treatments are required). Will your spouse be able to use the car? If not, can transport be arranged with other people when necessary? There may be things that you don't know, if only because you have never needed to discuss them previously. If the ill partner is the breadwinner and has been the financial organizer, you may not know how much money the family needs to cover costs, or even how much is available. You and your partner should spend time discussing these details, because you

will need this information to make a useful plan for the future.

4. *Get a Clear Idea of What Each of You Wants.* For instance, if the prognosis is gloomy and you may not have much "high-quality" time remaining, it is very important for each of you to indicate clearly what you would like. If you had been planning projects or trips together, discuss them. Planning for a short-term future may be awkward; it does, after all, involve abandoning hope. If you are both told that the illness is likely to be fatal in less than two years, hope may be one of the reactions you experience. Once you decide to take the trip you had been promising each other, you have begun accepting the gloomy prognosis. In my experience, many patients have a tendency to continue working because it helps them deny the illness. Sometimes they later regret that decision, wishing instead that they had stopped, to take the trip or enjoy some special time together.

The answer for you and your spouse is to make "What if . . ." plans. Discuss what you each would like to do *if* the doctor's prognosis is correct. This is a less threatening way of finding out what each of you really wants.

5. *List Your Resources.* Your list should include people, services, and money. Compare what each of you can now do with what you could do in the past. How big are the changes going to be? How much are your day-to-day arrangements going to have to change? Who should do what chores? For instance, while Anne was in the hospital, Bill — who had not previously done much of the housekeeping — arranged for Anne's parents to stay at their house. While all three were in a new situation, they planned in advance. This arrangement worked well from all points of view, including that of Bill and Anne's chil-

dren. Then, when Anne came home from the hospital, Bill arranged for a part-time leave of absence from his office. He went to the office for half a day, and did some of his work at home in the evenings. Again, because there was a good deal of discussion beforehand, the new situation caused very little panic. The children, although deeply affected by what was going on, nevertheless experienced a feeling that some continuity and calm was maintained in the household.

You can do the same. Do either of you have parents who could help with the children or come and stay? What about friends or brothers and sisters? Do you have insurance that includes nurse coverage? Are there neighbors that could take care of the children after school, until you get back from the hospital?

Talk together about finances. Many couples have never needed to have detailed conversations about money. However awkward it seems, find out how you both stand financially. Otherwise, sensible planning is impossible. You may want to speak to an accountant or other financial advisor, even if you haven't used one before. As with other plans, it is useful to decide which areas you can handle yourself, and which areas will benefit from other people's experience.

6. *Plan the Future for All Members of the Family*. Discuss plans for each member of the family, even though this is often painful. Of course, if you have children, planning for their future is of prime importance. Once you have made some overall plans for yourselves and for the children, it is often valuable to talk them over with the children. Try to reassure your children that many aspects of their life will continue uninterrupted. For instance, if you are sure that you will not have to sell the house, move out of town, or

change their schooling, let them know, giving them an important feeling of continuity.

Remember, as you make these plans, that *you, as survivor, do have a future*. Talking about this with your ill spouse will cause both of you pain. You will also feel a sense of guilt because you are thinking about a future in which he or she will not share. Do not let that feeling stop you from having these important conversations. Here is one example:

The patient says something like:

*"I want you to find someone
after I've died."*

↓

You have several choices:

↓   ↓

You can say: Or you can say:

↓

"Don't talk like that."   Nothing, just hold
                                            your spouse's hand.
        or
                                            — gives a special moment
"Let's not think about it."   of contact.

        ↓   or

These responses   "I'll never forget you."
close the door on
dialogue.   — which is what it's all
                                             about.

                                                   ↓

                                            This may lead you to
                                            show how what you
                                            have had together will
                                            always be a part of you.

7. *Plan One Step at a Time and Be Flexible*. The medical circumstances will change, your resources may change, your abilities may change. You will not be able to stick to a single plan made at the outset, and the need to change your plans should not worry you.

Problems with Sex

Talking about sexual problems that dying people may experience seems to break all the most powerful social taboos at once. It is a subject that everyone — patient, friend, doctor, and nurse alike — tries to avoid. But it is often of major importance. The sexual urge is a very powerful one for the great majority of people. It is one of the few urges that is powerful enough to sometimes serve as an antidote to pain and misery. Sex, for the seriously ill person, is sometimes the only readily accessible, if temporary, means of escape from the world of worry and misery in which she is enclosed. Not only is it a means of escape, it's a means of human contact and a means of achieving intimacy. It is also — because it's a normal activity — something that makes the patient feel like a normal human being, even if only for a moment.

However, sex can, and often does, go wrong when people are ill. In fact, specialists have found that sexual difficulties are almost universal among people who were sexually active at the time they became ill. Non-specialist doctors and nurses have not realized how common the problems are. They simply haven't asked. In fact, sexual difficulties add a great deal to the isolation, frustration, guilt, and rejection that are already the patient's lot. If you are the patient's sexual partner, or if either the patient or the patient's sexual partner can talk to you about sexual problems, there is much you can do to help.

Before considering what you can do, think about the factors that stop or obstruct sexual activity for you and the patient. Obstacles to sex come in two groups: the physical causes, and the emotional or psychological causes. Both can, of course, occur together.

The physical causes include anything that stops a couple from having sex when they both desire it. There are physical obstacles such as a catheter, surgery to the vagina or penis, injury to the nerves that cause male erection, and physical problems that may occur in the hips or lower back. There may be initial problems after bowel surgery, if there is a colostomy bag. Other problems may be of a more general medical nature, such as the pain of movement, or nausea or headache which is made worse during sexual activity.

Then there are less dramatic, if equally frustrating, unspoken physical barriers of being in a hospital. How are a couple supposed to have any form of sexual contact when one of them is an inpatient in a hospital? The answer, according to the unwritten law governing all hospital inpatients, is that they are not supposed to have any at all. ("That's not what hospitals are for!" as one senior nurse exclaimed when this subject was discussed at a seminar.)

Besides the physical problems that stop you when you do have the urge, many aspects of serious illness may eliminate the sexual urge itself. These may be affecting the patient, or you as the sexual partner.

Just feeling ill may decrease sex drive. While the sexual urge is quite powerful, biologically it's still something of a luxury that is apt to be jettisoned at times of medical emergency, particularly in stress and strain situations when the adrenaline-producing autonomic nervous system is overactive. Similarly, pain anywhere in the body — not just in the genital area — may decrease sexual appetite. Headaches in particular become worse during intercourse because pressure inside the skull rises during sexual excitement, increasing the pain.

Depression may also markedly decrease sex drive. In fact, this is so significant a sign of depression that psychiatrists use the loss of sexual appetite as an index of the severity of the depression. Many other feelings can do the same. The loss of self-confidence and self-esteem that may occur after breast surgery or with a colostomy may hamper the sex drive even if they don't directly affect sexual functioning. Similarly, the common shame and embarrassment of being ill and losing control of everything can reduce the patient's sexual confidence and impetus.

Emotional factors may affect you, the sexual partner. You might not find your friend attractive, due to the illness or some aspect of the treatment. After surgery it would be common for you to be afraid of doing harm. For example, after the patient has been given detailed instructions about what she may and may not do with the operation scar it's quite easy to regard your partner's body as "hospital property." I well remember one woman asking me, many months after the surgery, if I could get permission for her husband to touch her mastectomy scar. She was both surprised and relieved when I told her that her body was her property, not the surgeon's.

You might also have your own fears about sex with your loved one. Afraid that you will hurt him, you might find it difficult to believe him when he says he'd like to try anyway. Wondering whether you're causing pain makes it difficult to relax. You might also be afraid that if you are unable to perform sexually in your normal manner, your partner might sense that and take it as an insult, judgment, or rejection. You might be tempted to make an excuse and avoid the whole situation.

Sexual partners are often afraid of catching the disease, particularly when the patient has cancer. With AIDS, of course, such fears are justified and are the reason for practicing safe sex. With tumors, the unaffected partner can't catch the tumor. This is even true of some types of cancer of the cervix, which is caused by a particular effect of a certain type of virus on the cervix (particularly if acquired early in life). The virus is transmitted sexually, but of all the women who may become infected with the virus, only a very few will develop a cancer.

You might also be feeling angry or resentful. It is very difficult to evoke the trust and intimacy required for sex if you are angry at someone. In fact, denying your partner sexual gratification is a very common way of showing anger in any relationship.

There are, then, many reasons that sex goes wrong when people are ill. The result is further anger and frustration and guilt. Guilt, easily attached to sex at the best of times, is an especially likely outcome. The patient may feel guilty for making demands, for adding to the burden the healthy partner is already carrying. The healthy partner may feel guilty for denying something so clearly valuable to a seriously ill person. After her partner's death, she may feel guilty if she later enjoys another sexual relationship.

One woman I met had been unable to make love with her husband when he was dying of Hodgkin's disease. Though that was nearly twenty years previously, when she spoke to me the guilt was still so severe that she was unable to remember that time without crying. She had had con-

tinuous difficulties with sexual and emotional relationships ever since his death. Many partners have told me that
even when the patient felt well enough to regain interest in
sex, the lingering memory of the patient's illness affected
the physical attraction between them.

For all these reasons, then, sexual activity may be difficult. The following guide should help you tackle this
problem with sensitivity.

1. *Talk about It.* In my experience, a seriously ill or dying
person wants intimacy and human contact *even more than
sexual gratification itself.* If you cannot bring yourself to
join in sex, do not make up an excuse. Rather than blaming your lack of desire on some invented reason, talk about
your difficulty and listen to the patient's response. If you
feel tenderness and want to be intimate, but have a problem in showing those feelings sexually, say so. That in itself
is an expression of tenderness and concern that helps.

The illness or the treatment may change the patient's
appearance, making him unattractive to the partner. Re-
pelled by the patient's appearance, partners usually feel
very guilty. As a result, they often disguise their feelings.
This will not help. Feelings of physical repulsion are
neither uncommon nor abnormal. You must be honest and
sensitive at the same time. Talk about your feelings. Explain that your physical reaction to the patient's illness in
no way changes your feelings for your partner *as a person.*
These circumstances, more than any other problem with
sex, require of you a sensitive honesty.

2. *Be Specific about What You Can Do.* However embarrassing it might be to say so, talk about what you would be
prepared to do sexually. A cuddle or a hug can achieve a

great deal. Sometimes gratification for the patient alone —
masturbation — will help a lot. The extent of your ability
to help depends on you, and on your previous relationship
with the patient. But whatever you do, don't just ignore
the problem. Don't turn over and go to sleep (metaphori-
cally or literally), hoping that the problem will go away. It
will not. Unless you make some effort to confront the
problem, you may inadvertently saddle yourself with a
burden of guilt that could last for years, seriously affecting
your future sexual relationships.

If, as mentioned above, your partner's physical appearance has changed so that you are unable to be physically
excited by him, make it clear that you do not mind gratify-
ing him even if you are unable to be gratified yourself. This
can reduce the guilt for both of you. The intimacy of your
relationship can be restored, even if sexual intercourse cannot. One couple in their mid-fifties, Ralph and Susan, had
great difficulty coping with the sexual problems caused by
Ralph's bowel surgery. Initially, Susan felt repulsed by
Ralph's changed appearance. Ralph withdrew and then
became resentful. Once they were encouraged to talk
about it, they discovered that there was pleasure and
warmth to be found in what they could do. Susan had no
difficulty cuddling and kissing but she had previously
avoided that because she didn't want it to "lead on to
other things." The hugs and cuddles made Ralph feel less
rejected, and once Susan knew that she wasn't "expected"
to participate in intercourse she felt less tense and guilty.
Eventually, things improved so much that they were able
to perform mutual masturbation and then intercourse.
Their level of sexual activity was still considerably different from their previous level, but the damage to their emotional relationship was minimized.

Many couples wonder whether they should continue to sleep in the same bed. Many patients sleep with difficulty, due to pain, cough, or other symptoms, and it may be convenient for the healthy partner to sleep in a separate bed. This is a very important step, but it may increase the patient's sense of loneliness and isolation. If you are able to talk about sex and intimacy, you will be able to plan, for instance, to have sexual contact and then return to your own bed. This reduces your spouse's sense of rejection.

3. *Ask for Privacy.* On a purely practical level, some hospitals and nursing homes are adjusting to the idea that couples need undisturbed time together, with the unstated understanding that sex is a legitimate use of that time. Again, however embarrassing you may find it, ask a sympathetic nurse or doctor if a private room can be found, or if undisturbed time can be guaranteed. We've certainly organized that for couples on our units, if the patient simply cannot get home even for a night or a weekend. Be brave — ask.

4. *Get Help if You Need It.* You can get information about specific medical problems (including, for example, colostomies) from the relevant information groups. There are also resources available (booklets and video material) from professional associations dealing with sexual counseling. You will find some helpful addresses at the end of this book.

After the Bereavement

Starting life again after the loss of your spouse is a daunting prospect. There are many books written specifically on this subject by widows and widowers who have been through the experience and have valuable hints and tips to offer. The following steps need emphasis:

1. *Accept the Way You Feel.* Do not drive yourself with the need to be "strong." Instead, allow yourself to acknowledge and express your emotions as you have in the past.

2. *Assess Your Needs.* You may now have needs that you have not had to consider previously, because they were your partner's responsibility. You should think about all aspects of your life (and this is where reading one of the specialized books on the subject can be most helpful).

3. *List Your Resources.* There are often more resources available than you first realize. These may include other family members, friends, social services, financial supports, associations, clubs, and local organizations.

4. *Don't Make Big Decisions Rapidly.* Particularly if your spouse's illness was prolonged, you may have spent a long time without close companionship, intimacy, and sex. Your needs may be many, and the sense of relief that often occurs at the end of a partner's long illness may push you to seek comfort with other partners. While there is nothing wrong with this, you should not make any long-term decisions rapidly. Your sense of balance and perspective are likely to be badly affected and you may not be capable of making the best choice for you. As Ruth put it very succinctly, "For the short-term the message is 'date, but don't marry.'" The same is true of all major decisions at this difficult time.

5. *Get Help if You Need It.* As I've already mentioned, you need to decide whether you are making progress in

your grief or not. If, as the months pass, your pain maintains its intensity, if you cannot think of the person you have lost without crying, and if you are not beginning to function more normally in your day-to-day life, then you may need help, and you should seek some expert advice. There is no set time course for the completion of grief: if you are making even slow progress you should feel encouraged; if you are not making progress, you should get help.

LOSING A BROTHER OR SISTER

Relationships between brothers and/or sisters are even more varied than marriages. Some siblings are so close ("blood is thicker than water") that their intuitive understanding of each other's feelings may appear telepathic to outsiders. Others have a great deal of affection for each other even if they do not meet often. Others are not even friends, and some are frankly antagonistic and openly competitive. Generalizations are therefore difficult.

However, what siblings have in common, whether they like it or not, is a shared past. Research has shown that if siblings are close in age (less than three years' difference) they spend, on average, more time in each other's company than with their parents. Hence, even if they grow apart as they grow older, many siblings have a fund of shared experience that may be more intimate and more secret than the past shared with their parents.

Furthermore, your sibling represents your generation. The threat of a sibling's death, therefore, may make you feel very vulnerable. Depending on your relationship to your sibling, you may be shattered by the illness or (if you are totally antagonistic) relieved that it is not happening to you.

There are few general guidelines that cover all the variations on sibling relationships. However, the following are points that are worth bearing in mind:

1. *Think about Your Relationship to Date.* It's worth pausing for a moment or two to think about what you have meant to each other up to now. It's a peculiar thing to think about, and most brothers and sisters don't have to try it; but if your sibling is dying, you should try to assess the strength and intimacy of your relationship.

2. *Think about Your Role.* Depending on the nature of your relationship, you may be a key person in the support of your sibling, or you may be on the fringe. Where you are in your sibling's circle of support does not matter as long as you *know* your position, and make plans that are appropriate for your particular relationship. Quite often, a patient can get more support from a sibling than from anyone else. I remember one patient, Barb, whose younger sister Julie formed the hub of Barb's whole circle. Besides resembling one another, Julie and Barb were great friends. Julie kept in touch with Barb's circle of friends and relatives. She organized Barb's husband and their children, and gave Barb an enormous amount of support, bringing her the tangible relief of knowing that her dependents were being cared for. Of course, not every sibling relationship has the potential to be strong and caring, but often bonds do exist that can be a major source of support.

3. *Use the Past.* Whatever your current relationship, the past can be a common bond now. Reminiscence can be the

first step to bringing you closer together, to establishing a supportive relationship where one might not exist already.

4. *Accept the Person as He or She Is.* Remind yourself of the principles mentioned in the section on parents at the beginning of this chapter. Acceptance means that you have to stop trying to change the other person, or expecting them to change. If you have been separated, this is a time for mending fences, *not* settling scores. If you are close, build on your strengths by drawing on the material in this book.

LOSING A FRIEND

Friends, like siblings, usually represent our peers — our generation. A dying friend means not only the loss of someone near but also a warning that we, too, are mortal. This intimation of mortality often frightens people. You may want to keep your distance from this dying friend, rather than confront the fact that you yourself are not immune from dying. Staying away is often the outward sign of denial on the part of the supporting circle of friends.

Sometimes, friendship reaches great levels of intimacy. This is more common among women than among men, for as Ruth puts it, when talking about women's friendships: "Many of us have friends with whom we exchange things we don't with anybody else. I am not talking about secrets, but about a depth of knowing each other and sharing that is, in a way, more intimate than we have with any family member. We see each other or talk to each other every day, and the loss of that kind of friend would be a huge blow."

As a friend, therefore, you might be privy to a special part of the patient's personality. You might also be in a better position to help than many of the family members.

There are many things that a non-family member can do easily for the patient, because the relationship is based on equality. You can often spend time with the spouse of the patient, or relieve the spouse at home so that he can spend time with the patient. You can spend time listening to other family members and you may be able to mediate any squabbles and arguments that commonly arise under these stressful conditions. Very often a close friend acts as a combination of spouse, sibling, and parent. You can be a very powerful source of support and help.

YOUNG CHILDREN

Young children dying, or young children confronting the death of someone else in the family, present special problems. In this section I shall first confront the problems facing and surrounding a young child who is dying, and then consider the problems of a young child facing the death of another family member or close friend.

The Dying Child

Whenever I think of the sad subject of children and dying, my most vivid image is always of one particular boy, Simon, who was eleven years old when I first met him. A tumor in the spinal cord had caused paralysis of his legs and trunk. He could use his arms but the tumor (a very rare one) had come back after treatment and it was expected that he would live only a few months. Intellectually, he was very bright, and, although as a patient he wasn't assigned to me, I used to play Scrabble with him (an educational experience for me, since he was the better player). I didn't know how much he knew about the illness, and since I was only an "outsider" I didn't talk to him about the illness at all. But one day, when he'd put down some particularly smart word on the Scrabble board, I asked (more as a joke than anything else), "How old *are* you, Simon?" He looked straight at me, and said, "I am eleven years four months and three days old." I had no idea of how to respond, and I couldn't think of anything to say, so I just sat there feeling very awkward until he added, "And I am dying inch by inch."

Not every child has such a clear vision of what is happening, but I learned then to never underestimate a child's comprehension.

The subject itself is colossal. I will start by summarizing the way in which a child's understanding of the meaning of death changes with age and maturity. Then I shall deal with the reaction of parents to losing a child, and then go on to offer some guidelines for a practical approach to coping with the huge losses involved.

A Child's Understanding of Death at Different Ages

Most children under five years have very little comprehension of the true meaning of dying. This is partly because they do not have a sense of time as adults know it. For a small child, the concept of "next month" or "next year" has very little meaning. Very young children with serious illnesses are not usually preoccupied with their own death. They are generally much more concerned with whether or not their parents are spending time with them. Thus, most dying young children think less of themselves than of the frightening possibility that their parents might not be available when needed. In fact, one of the major tasks in a child's early development is learning the idea that people return. Allowing Mommy out of sight, for even a few minutes, without anxiety is the sign that a toddler is learning this principle.

A young child who is dying will be reassured by having her family around, and may not require the help that adults need to cope with the abstract idea of dying.

Children between the ages of six and ten are generally aware that dying means forever, but still lack a solidly based view of their own future. Thus, although they are much more concerned with the present than is the toddler, they do not usually spend much time contemplating the future. Instead they react more strongly to the limitations imposed by the disease or treatment. They want to know about the illness, and why it stops them from doing the things they want.

Teenagers, on the other hand, are much more likely to resent their shortened life. As a child grows into his teens, he is likely to discover his own talents and have some image of his own potential. He may have decided on a possible career or a major hobby. He may have discovered that he is good at one particular sport or subject at school. As he begins to understand his own personal potential, so he will regret the loss of what might have been, and this can be a tragic and bitter experience, both for the young patient and for the family members who support him. It is this realization of wasted potential, and the accompanying bitterness, that often causes seriously ill teenagers to express their emotions in rebellious actions, such as failing to take medications or ignoring medical advice. Acting out one's rebellion in this manner is a common reaction to major life changes at this stage.

After describing the reactions of the parent, I shall offer a scheme by which you can assess your child's understanding of what is going on, and then try to match the support to the child's needs.

A Parent's Reaction to a Dying Child

For most parents, the possible death of their child is the most terrifying loss imaginable. The pain that parents suffer is almost impossible to describe. When a parent says, "I wish I could change places, have this illness, and die in place of my child," there's no doubt in my mind that she means it.

Many powerful emotional elements combine to make this pain so deep. First, the biological bond between parent and child is exceptionally strong. One of the major forces that ensures the survival of every species, the "animal" instincts pulling the parent toward the threatened child are necessarily strong and deep.

Second, there are the bonds of responsibility. You may feel that since you brought the child into the world, the responsibility must be yours if the child is ill or dying. Partly instinctive and partly biological, this guilty feeling of responsibility is not easily quelled.

Added to the sense of responsibility is the sensation of helplessness. Finding that you are unable to fix what goes wrong when you've been able to fix so many things before can create another major source of guilt.

Added to these are the more social and philosophical elements of your pain. Children are not meant to die before their parents. It seems unnatural. However naive that may sound, many parents have said to me that a dying child challenges their whole view of the way the world is supposed to work. Derek and Suzanne, whose son, James, died of a rare bone tumor, put it this way: "A young child dying is a fundamental insult to your whole idea of the structure of the world, as a parent. It knocks you sideways. It makes you feel that your whole idea about everything around you has been wrong. It's worse than unfair — it's almost obscene." As Derek and Suzanne say, this force is a very deep one — and actually it is no less powerful when the child is not young. Parents feel similarly challenged even if they are in their seventies and the child is in his fifties.

There is also the strong feeling that childhood is supposed to be a time of joy and protected pleasure. Illness belongs to the adult world, something suffered when we can understand and handle it. Illness in childhood is grossly unfair, a brutal assault on an innocent.

These feelings run very deep. And when a child dies, the desire to find someone to blame is very strong. Parents commonly have a strong urge to blame one another, and often find themselves in a series of "if only you had . . ." and "why didn't you . . ." arguments.

It is very important for all parents in this tragic situation to be aware that the risk of divorce after the death of a child is very high. It becomes increasingly easy to hate and blame one another for what has occurred, and, later on, equally easy to associate the marriage with the damage and destruction of the child's life. As a result, there is often a strong desire to get away from the whole thing, to start again.

If you are in this position, try to understand the various forces tearing at you. If you can understand that the anger and rage you may be experiencing are neither your nor your partner's fault, perhaps you can limit the damage to your relationship. You may well need help. Talk to each other, of course, but don't hesitate to get help from outside. There are counselors, therapists, and self-help groups of bereaved parents who've been through the experience and know what it is like. Many people can help, but none of them will be of value to you if you do not seek their assistance. And you won't go to them if you genuinely believe that it's all your partner's fault (or yours), if you exhaust yourself in blame, rage, and regret.

Perhaps the most vivid example of this is what happened to David and Patricia. Their first son, Chris, suffered from a very rare metabolic disease which resulted in his death at the age of nine. Two years before Chris died, their younger son, Robert, was found to be suffering from the same condition (though the chance of this happening was very low — one in several million). David told me that the strain on the marriage was immense and indescribable. After their first son died, they sought counseling. With the right sort of help, David and Patricia stayed together and maintained support for each other through the death of their second child. Neither of them believed beforehand that they could have coped with this terrible burden, but with help they did, and they now have a normal and healthy third child — and a very successful marriage.

HOW TO MAKE PRACTICAL PLANS

1. *Become Informed.* As I have mentioned previously, you do need information to make effective plans, but you should not try to become an expert on your child's disease. The sense of outrage and impotence at the seemingly arbitrary course of events often drives parents to accumulate great amounts of information. They assume that "there must be something that somebody hasn't thought of." Sadly, time spent doing this is time denied to the child, often adding desperation to a situation already fraught with tension.

2. *Find Out What Your Child Understands.* This means you must listen carefully to what the child is saying and the questions your child is asking. Don't assume that all words mean the same for the child as they do for you. Check

by asking your child what they mean. For instance, Julie, a six-year-old girl with childhood leukemia, asked her mother, while I was with them: "When will I feel better?" The mother was very upset because she thought that the question was about the long-term future. In fact, Julie just wanted to know how long she would have nausea from the chemotherapy (which, in her case, was eventually successful). By asking Julie what she meant, I was able to give a direct answer. In the same way, if your child asks you about dying, find out what she understands before trying to answer in your own terms.

On that subject, you must be prepared to answer the same questions time and time again. This is a part of the way younger children learn and retain things, and it is also reassuring for the child to hear the same answers to the same questions. This provides an element of consistency in a threatening situation and may actually be comforting for the child, even though it may be hard on you.

3. *Make a List of Your Resources.* Think about what each member of the family can and is prepared to do. Will the other children take turns visiting the hospital? Can older children or other relatives make meals for younger children or the sick child? If the child is out of the hospital, think about the possible ways of spending valuable time together. Your child might want to spend some in a "normal" environment for a child his age. In many parts of the United States there are holiday camps specifically for children with serious illnesses. Would your child want to spend some time there? What can each of you do to help the child spend time doing his favorite things (sports, hobbies, computers, for instance)?

It's a good idea to gather your friends around you. They may be somewhat unwilling, because the death of a child always arouses strong feelings. Even if that's the case, see if they can help you indirectly. If your child is in the hospital, for instance, perhaps your friends can stay at your home while you visit.

4. *Try to Find Out What Is Best for Your Child.* The secret in making the most appropriate plan is not to try to cram a whole life's worth of experience into the short time available. Tempted as you are to show your child as much of the world as possible, remember that for most children the world consists of family, friends, and the neighborhood. Certainly, try to widen the range of your child's experience somewhat, but *don't do anything too grandiose.* A few short trips and local visits are better than the upheaval of a massive excursion, particularly if the child is physically frail. Sometimes simply staying home with the family is of greater support and reassurance than a big excursion.

5. *Make Plans for the Other Family Members as Well.* Don't forget the other family members — particularly other children. Healthy siblings of a dying child often feel angry that they are being ignored. The sick child seems to be "getting all the attention." They know that this feeling is "wrong," and they may feel guilty about it. You can avoid a lot of this by keeping the other children informed about what's going on (thereby making them feel part of the family again), and by reserving exclusive time for them. For instance, don't neglect the other children's school-work. Help them to make cards for their sick sibling. Make them feel involved, not excluded. The same is often true of other relatives — even your spouse. A child's illness can make the less-involved spouse feel insecure, jealous, and resentful. Include him in your plans at each stage.

Remember that nobody likes being told what to do if they don't know why they're supposed to do it.

6. *Try to Keep Life as Normal as Possible.* Everything is changing for your child because of her medical condition. If possible, keep the general tenor of your family life on an even keel. This is very hard to achieve, and the tendency to lurch from crisis to crisis is common. But wherever you can, try to maintain some semblance of normality for your child. Read the usual bedtime stories, even if you are in the hospital with the child. Watch the usual television programs and talk about them together wherever you happen to be. Try to prepare some of your child's familiar meals, whether at home or hospital, even if your child has a poor appetite — the routine provides a bit of comfort for you both. Wherever you can, introduce a note of familiarity: decorate, for instance, the child's bedside table with her own ornaments, or buy the usual magazines, or rent the family's favorite videos.

TALKING AND LISTENING

As I have already indicated with the story of Simon at the start of this section, many children's mature understanding of their plight may exceed an adult's expectations. We all, as adults, tend to lower the level of the discussion when we are talking with children about painful subjects. Subconsciously, we hope that the child will not understand the situation fully, so that we are spared the pain of discussing it with him.

While you are talking with and listening to your child, you need to employ all the techniques of sensitive listening that I have mentioned before. Pay special attention to the following:

1. *Pick Your Moment.* Sometimes, in an emergency, you have to talk immediately. Usually, however, you can pick your moment. Bedtime, or during a car journey, are times that are relatively free of distraction, whereas if you interrupt a favorite television program or a game in which your child is engrossed, you will not get his full attention and you will probably irritate him.

2. *Remember That the Concentration Span of Children Is Short.* Depending on your child's age and previous abilities, she may only be able to concentrate fully for a short time. Ten minutes is a very long time for small children, and even for teenagers. It is always better (where possible) to have a few short conversations rather than one long one. You should also be prepared to have the same conversation several times, because retention may be limited and the child may enjoy the same conversation as reassurance.

3. *Check to Make Sure How Much Is Getting Through.* Try not to give long chunks of explanation without asking if he is understanding it, and try to get him to tell you what he does understand. Substance is most often better than a glib phrase. "One day I'll explain it all" accomplishes little unless you've already given a fair amount of information that is not making sense to the child. One child, Andrew, got so used to hearing his father say, "One day I'll explain it all," that he finally asked, "Daddy, when will it be 'one day'?" His father responded well, and discovered that having the promised conversation was much less of a problem than he had feared.

I shall give one example of the options available when a child asks a hard question. Many of the things that children ask when they are seriously ill can be very painful for you, but you should respond with honesty and consistency to avoid making the situation worse.

The patient says something like:

"When am I going to get better?"

You have several choices:

You could say:

"Ask the doctor."

or

"Wait and see."

— and lose some of your
ability to support
your child by
"ducking out" when
your help is needed.

Or you could say:

"Soon."

— then, if he doesn't feel
better, he won't
trust you.

Or you could say:

*"Soon you won't have any
more pain."*

— which may not be
understandable to a
child.

Or you could say:

*"If we could make you
better, we would."*

— which is truthful, and
may lead the child to
ask:

*"Why can't you make me
better?"*

This allows you to say:

*"Sometimes there are
things that nobody can
fix, no matter how much
they would like to."*

Holding this kind of dialogue with your child is tough, and most parents will not have any experience to guide them. Other health services can help you if they are available. (Many pediatric units have child psychologists or experienced social workers attached to the unit.)

If there are no other people at hand, books can help. Many books have been specifically written for children who at different ages and stages are facing serious illness. There are some books, usually written for health professionals, but useful for parents as well, on talking to children about the subject of death. Books can be a useful adjunct to the help of an experienced professional. Some of the more useful books are listed in the Recommended Reading list at the end of this book.

After the Bereavement

Grief after the loss of a child is always intense, and often deep and prolonged. Besides my earlier description of the course of grief, these additional points can help you stabilize yourself and your family after the death of a child.

1. *Try Not to Idealize.* The death of a child does mean a vast loss of potential, but it is very easy to slip into a habit of idealizing him. Expressions such as, "He was always the brightest" or, "I'm sure she would have been a brilliant scientist or writer or musician" may not help you keep close to the reality of the loss. They may also make surviving siblings feel unwanted and second-rate. Try not to imagine too much from the life that was lost.

2. *Don't Cling to Objects for Too Long.* After the death, it's hard to know what to get rid of. The child's toys and

clothes may provide a form of contact or reminder (they are called "transitional objects") but as grief does its work you should be able to let go of them. Again, there's no fixed timetable for this, but if, several months later, you're still clinging to the child's things rather than making progress with your pain and sorrow, you should think seriously about getting some help. When you feel able, you should perhaps change the child's room into something neutral like a guest room or a den. Avoid making a shrine of it. Avoid "this was always Johnny's favorite chair."

3. *Don't Make Big Decisions Quickly.* Just as widows should avoid getting married on the rebound, so you and your partner should not plan your future life too quickly after such massive loss. *Don't decide instantly to have another child.* Some couples make this decision quickly, hoping that "to replace the one that's died" will abolish the pain of their grieving. Sadly, that does not work. No child ever replaces one that was lost, because every child is an individual. To think otherwise is unfair to the next child, and very hard for you.

4. *Share Your Grief Selectively.* You cannot disguise your grief totally from your partner, or from other children you might have. But, to some extent, you can control the manner in which you express that grief. With your partner you can explain how you feel in detail, but with the children it is important to try to express your grief in understandable terms ("I feel sad because Robin has died, but I won't always be sad"). It is most important that you pick your words carefully when you talk about the child who has died. "He's gone to sleep forever," for instance, may make the surviving children frightened to go to sleep, in case they die, too.

5. *Don't Hesitate to Ask for Help.* The divorce rate among couples who have lost a child is high. Both of you may be trying to minimize the extent of your loss for the benefit of other children, relatives, and each other. While this feeling is natural and appropriate, you should not ignore your own deep feelings. Your marriage will not feel the same after the bereavement, but if it does not seem to be coming back together again after a few months, seek help. A divorce or separation is doubly hard for the surviving children after a bereavement, and with the appropriate help you may be able to avoid it.

THE CHILD'S RESPONSE TO THE DEATH OF A PARENT

In the first part of this section, I shall deal with the child's reaction to a terminally ill parent. In the second part, I shall discuss the problems facing the child and you after the parent's death.

Children and a Parent's Illness

During a parent's severe illness, a child's response will to some extent be determined by his ability to understand what is going on. A little child may ask, "When is Mommy going to get better?" Even if he is told, "Mommy is never going to get better," he may still be unable to associate this concept with Mother never being there. He will, however, be aware that his parent is sick, in pain, and not the way she used to be. This may cause an intense reaction, one sometimes directed against the sick patient. Fears of abandonment and guilt may well start before the death. If the parent is being looked after at home, the child may feel guilty and unhappy that he cannot make his parent feel better. He may feel jealous of the amount of time and attention the healthy parent spends taking care of the patient. He may also be frightened by the appearance of his ill parent, or upset by tubes, apparatus, smells, or sights, all of which require explanation to the child in understandable terms. With adequate explanation and preparation, a great deal can be achieved. One couple, John and Sharon, had a daughter, Mandy, who was seven when John became terminally ill with a rare sarcoma. Mandy was a very bright and intelligent child, and both John and Sharon had remarkable emotional strength. The stability of that family was so great that on the day John died, I saw Mandy sitting quietly by his bedside (while John was wearing an oxygen mask) coloring a card for him and drawing pictures. That was several years ago, and I still keep in touch with Sharon and Mandy. Surely, her family's calm and caring approach to her father's death has contributed to Mandy's excellent intellectual growth and emotional development.

Practical Tips

1. *Never Make a Child Do Something She Does Not Want to Do.* Instead, try to understand what is behind the refusal — it will usually be anxiety or fear. Remember that children tend to express their emotions in actions rather than in words. If they refuse to visit the hospital it may be because they are frightened of the hospital, of the illness, or of not knowing what to say. Encourage your child to tell the sick parent about school and friends. It is usually easy for the child to talk about these things, and reassuring for the ill parent.

2. *Keep Visits Short for Small Children.* Try to time the visits so that they coincide with the patient's most comfortable time of day (just after pain medication has been given, for instance). If the parent is stuporose or unconscious, allow the child just a short visit, and reassure him that the parent is no longer in pain.

3. *Include and Involve Your Child with Activities.* It is useful for your child to make cards for the ill parent, to paint pictures, to write notes, and to see those notes displayed by the bedside. It reminds the child that she is a valued member of the family. Bring games and other play items to the hospital so that the patient can have some interaction with the child.

4. *Expect Responses and Don't Panic.* Do not be frightened if your child screams "I hate Mommy" or "I never want to see her again." The child is experiencing a tremendous sense of loss and outrage at the abandonment. Do not criticize the child, but see if you can make him understand that seeing Mommy unwell is hard on all the family. Do not confront the child, or force him to behave well at this stage; just stay close. A child who shows no response whatever to a very ill parent has probably got a bigger problem than a child who reacts openly.

5. *List Your Resources.* As at any stage, with any situation, you may need help — and the more support your child has, the better.

6. *Let the School Know.* Since the child's behavior or performance at school may well be affected by what is going on, it is important that you let the school know so that they can make reasonable allowance for changes. More

importantly, they can let you know of any big changes in behavior.

7. *Reserve Time for the Children.* It doesn't need to be much, but it does need to be consistent. You may feel the need to be at the sick parent's bedside every night and on weekends, but try to arrange for some relief so that you can spend time with your children. You cannot make up for it later. They will need you later, but they also need you now.

After the Death of a Parent

For a young child, the death of a parent (particularly the mother) has a major effect. Most children will go through several different and intense emotions, the most important of which are guilt and a sense of abandonment. Obviously a child losing a parent will feel a sense of being abandoned ("Why did Daddy leave me?"), but the origins of her guilt may be less obvious. Most parents underestimate the amount of guilt a young child may experience as a result of an event which, so obviously, is no fault of the child's.

Children feel guilty because they are accustomed to being punished for doing things they did not realize would cause problems ("You left your shoes at the bottom of the stairs and I tripped on them"). Hence, when a major event occurs, they search for things that *they* might have done wrong which may have caused it. "Perhaps" — a child might think — "if I'd tidied my room like she told me, Mom would have got better." This point is crucial to understanding how a child perceives the loss of a parent.

It is also important to remember that children often express their emotions in actions rather than in words.

Watch for abrupt changes in behavior. This may be the only sign of what your child is truly feeling. Important changes in behavior include sudden changes in performance at school, inability to pay attention, changes in tidiness, bed-wetting, or reverting to bad habits of the past.

The key to helping your child after a bereavement is to be as consistent as you can. A fixed point of the child's universe has disappeared. Deeply insecure now, the child will be wondering whether you are about to disappear, too. You should therefore do everything you can to show your child clearly that you are *not* going to abandon her. And you should get help if the situation does not improve as time goes on.

The following guidelines offer some practical tips to help you avoid the most common pitfalls.

A GUIDE TO GIVING SUPPORT

1. *Be Consistent.* Make special efforts to show that you are not going to disappear from your child's world. Show that you are there for your child, and that you have every intention of staying. Of course, you cannot say, "I'm never going to die," but you can say, "I'm not going to die until you're old yourself and have children of your own." Make small contracts and stick to them. If you say you'll be back at five o'clock, make certain that you are. Do everything to reduce uncertainty for your child. Try never to let him down or go back on a promise. Don't cheat. Don't go out in the evening without telling him, leaving him with a baby-sitter and hoping he will sleep through. The consequences of being let down by the remaining parent are large.

After a bereavement, many children wake in the night and come to sleep in their parent's bed. If you can, let the child snuggle in beside you, and then return him to his own bed while he is asleep. In this way he will not feel rejected by you, but will still wake up in his own bed. Many childhood fears return after bereavement. You may be asked to leave a night-light on, when previously the child was content to sleep without one. Small amounts of regressive behavior (even including occasional bed-wetting) are common and quite normal. Provided there isn't a large or prolonged change in habits, this can be accepted as a normal response to bereavement.

2. *Make Time for Your Child.* Make it clear that there are times when you are totally available for your child. Even if the child does not take up your offer and, for instance, plays downstairs while you are upstairs, knowing that you are there is important. Stopping all aspects of your normal life in order to devote yourself entirely to your child only adds to the "abnormality" of your situation. But you should increase your "special" time, however it is actually spent.

3. *Find Out What's Going On.* Watch out for big changes in behavior. Ask your child's teachers at school how she is doing with her subjects and when she is playing with other children. If your child's teachers don't know about the parental loss, they may not be on the lookout for signs of disturbance. Likewise, if you do not ask them, they cannot help you. Ask the parents of other children to let you know if they see or hear of any very unusual behavior on the part of your child. Naturally, you do not want to create an atmosphere of suspicion where small details are overblown, but you do not want to miss something big.

4. *Get Help if You Need It.* In most households, the death of one parent makes major demands on the surviving parent's time, finances, availability, and energy. You cannot do everything alone that the two of you did before. Make a list of your needs and get help to match it with a list of your resources. You may need simple things, such as baby-sitters or cooking or housework help, or you may need special help with your child's educational and psychological needs. For your child's sake, don't be afraid to ask.

If you do need professional help from a counselor or psychotherapist, there are many different ways of finding out what is available. In some areas there are self-help groups devoted to bereaved families. These usually offer group support and/or counseling, and can usually provide the names of the most experienced therapists specializing in grief and bereavement. Otherwise, you can ask your family practitioner, the pediatrics department at the local hospital, any of the social services, or the administration of the local hospital or disease-specific agency (such as the American Cancer Society).

5. *Keep Your Roles Clear.* After a parental loss, a child may try to "become" the lost parent in order to fill the gap. A daughter may want to run the home, becoming, in the process, the mother who has died. This occurs quite frequently. This is good in the sense that the daughter feels needed and wanted, and feels that she is reducing the impact of the loss on the family. But it can endanger the normal growth and development of the child. If a daughter of, say, nine or ten years old becomes the housewife, replacing the mother and caring for the other children, her own teen growth and development can be difficult. A further problem will arise if, at a later date, you wish to

remarry or introduce another adult into the family. Then you will be replacing, and apparently rejecting, the child in her "new" role.

If your child does attempt to take the place of the parent who has died, you should, however valuable and useful that help may seem in the short term, talk it over with someone experienced in child guidance and therapy.

TALKING AND LISTENING

1. *Try to Deal with Guilt before It Becomes a Problem.* Reinforce as often as you can the fact that the parent who died did not *want* to leave the family. You need to stress the fact that some things happen that are *nobody's* fault, that cannot be avoided or fixed by adults, no matter how willing or capable. When Leslie died, Ruth achieved this by drawing a special book for her young son, Michael. It showed a family of birds, in which the father bird was killed accidentally and the mother bird and baby bird lived in the nest alone. This became Michael's favorite book, and he would read it to his toys, explaining death to them. It was very hard, and sad, for adult relatives to hear him do this and to maintain a smiling and interested face while he did, but it removed all elements of guilt, allowing Michael a very early acceptance of what had happened. There are several commercially available children's books that deal with the loss of a parent.

2. *Don't Shy away from Reminiscence.* The parent who has died was an important part of your child's life, and it is foolish and dangerous to pretend otherwise. One patient of mine, Frances, was widowed in her early thirties. She removed everything from the house that related to her husband, who had died suddenly. His name was not men-

tioned, there was no grieving within the family, and life instantly started up without him. While this did allow Frances to get on with her own life almost immediately, her children, who had no opportunity to grieve and nobody to whom they could talk about their father, had an extremely difficult time. A great deal of strain was created within the family, and, in some respects, her sons have never quite adjusted to her attitude. It is almost as if they have not quite "forgiven" her for sweeping their father's memory away so completely and rapidly. Their relationship with their mother has never been as close as it was before their father's death.

You should not, therefore, shy away from reminiscence with other family members. Keep the photos and videos or films you may have, particularly if they show the child with the deceased parent in an affectionate or happy scene. If you find the pictures too painful to look at yourself, put them in an album so that your child can look at them. While it is sad to recall the good times when your spouse is gone, it is far better to do that, and to accept your loss, than to pretend you have no memories at all.

3. *Share Your Grief Appropriately*. You neither can nor should totally conceal your own grief from your child. Trying to hide your true feelings will simply make your child feel excluded and rejected. On the other hand, the *way* you express your grief is quite important. Use language the child can understand and be specific about its meaning ("Sometimes I feel sad when I think about Daddy, and I miss him, but I love you and I'll feel better soon"). You should shield your child from the undiluted force of your own despair. Don't say anything like, "I feel so terrible that I don't know how I'm going to cope."

In talking about your own feelings you should also be

aware that your child might experience anger. The anger is usually directed at the parent who has died. The child is often angry at having been abandoned. This can be made worse if you or anyone else tries to reduce the child's pain by painting a very bright picture of an afterlife. "Mommy's gone to a lovely place where she's very happy" will only increase the child's sense of abandonment.

A CHILD'S RESPONSE
TO THE DEATH OF A SIBLING

The death of a brother or sister is devastating, particularly if the siblings were close in age and spent a lot of time together. The surviving child will feel lonely and confused. She may spend a lot of energy trying to work out why the dead sibling was the one "chosen" to die. This can be made worse if you idealize or glorify the child who has died, even if you have the best intentions ("Your brother Bobby was always so good, and so cheerful"). The surviving sibling may feel very guilty that she is still alive when the "good" one has died, and may develop low self-esteem. As with the death of a parent, the child may also think of and talk about joining the child who has died. This is not common, but if it does happen you should get some help.

In summary then, what I'm saying about children and dying is that there are some specific factors to be aware of. Talk to children at the right level — which means talking, listening, and asking — and try to remember that they may go through any number of different emotions as they try to make sense of the idea of dying. And, finally, don't hesitate to get help. A death in the family is devastating for you and even more so for the children. Getting help now, when the problems are beginning, is a lot easier than leaving it until later.

12

AIDS and Demeting Diseases

🐎 Support of the dying person is particularly difficult when the patient has AIDS, or when a disease involves the loss of mental capacity.

In practice, the "special" nature of the disease is not very important. All the processes described in previous chapters still go on, and what works to improve communication between patient and friend will still work, whether the patient has cancer of the breast, motoneuron disease, or AIDS.

There are, however, certain social factors which can make the supporter's task more difficult, and in this chapter I'm going to focus on those.

AIDS

You probably don't need reminding that AIDS is a disease of the immune system caused by a virus. The virus can be transmitted sexually in body fluids, by contaminated needles used by addicts, by blood transfusions (before screening became routine), and by the mother to the fetus inside the womb. The virus itself is rather weak and easily killed outside the body. It cannot be transmitted by casual contact, or by contact with objects that have been handled by AIDS patients. Once infected with the virus, the patient may or may not develop the disease itself. If the disease does develop, it renders the patient prone to many different kinds of infections, including certain kinds of pneumonias that are rare in the unaffected population. The virus also makes the patients prone to certain kinds of tumors, including a cancer of the skin called Kaposi's sarcoma, and cancer of the lymph glands called lymphoma (this is a fairly common tumor — most patients with lymphoma do not have AIDS). The most important thing to remember — and it is hard to hold on to facts when there is so much hysteria and overreaction — is that you can't catch AIDS by casual contact with a patient if you are not exposed to the patient's blood. If you have a friend with AIDS, you won't catch it by visiting him.

But because the homosexual population is the most readily identifiable group at high risk of developing AIDS, many social pressures are added to the burden of the AIDS patient and friends. Fear and distrust of homosexuals — a social phenomenon known as homophobia — is fairly deeply rooted in many cultures. Like all fears of a group that can be easily identified, it is an easy fear to whip up and exploit. In that respect, homophobia is similar to racism, or anti-Semitism. It is not difficult to convince some part of the population that they are Us, and that another group is a distinct Them. That has always been a quick and easy way to raise a great deal of distrust and fear. If you can show that They have a disease because of something They do, and that They are therefore a threat to Us, you

can fuel the fire with self-justified rage. This is the rea-
soning that calls AIDS the "gay plague" and suggests that
it is a visitation by God. It is so much more difficult to
identify, on the other hand, smokers as They, despite the
fact that They (smokers) die in much larger numbers than
do AIDS victims, and that They are a threat to Us (non-
smokers) in the form of passive smoking. I suppose the
difference between smoking habits and sexual practices
lies in the social taboos and embarrassments surrounding
sex, so that there is a ready-made source of fear and ignorance easy to ignite against AIDS victims.

An AIDS sufferer finds himself on the other side of the
fence from Us. Many AIDS patients are denied the common social charity and sympathy they could expect were
they suffering from, say, multiple sclerosis or arthritis. It is
almost as if the suffering of a homosexual AIDS patient
isn't *really* suffering at all, because "he brought it on himself." This is an attitude that nobody would dream of ap-
plying to a person with lung cancer from smoking, or to a
teenager paralyzed from the neck down because she was
driving while intoxicated.

In some respects, AIDS occupies the position in our society occupied by syphilis a century ago. Then, syphilis was
the vengeful killer punishing Those who had Strayed, even
reaching down to strike their children. (The Ibsen plays
Ghosts and *A Doll's House* both have characters struck
down by syphilis as a judgment on them.) The disease was
invested with an aura of mysticism and divine retribution.
Now that we know syphilis is caused by a bacterium and is
(in the vast majority of cases) curable by antibiotics, it is
merely a serious infection. Exactly the same was true of
tuberculosis until the 1940s. It may be that in years to
come AIDS will be controlled by safe sexual practices and

by vaccination, perhaps even by treatment, in which case it, too, will lose most of its mystical significance.

Until then AIDS is a disease that puts its victims into a special category — one that some people think should prevent them from getting the kind of humane treatment any other sick person claims as a right. As a result, AIDS patients are not only facing the social taboos associated with death and dying, but must also confront the other taboos of homosexuality and immorality, adding to the already heavy burden of facing death at a young age.

Their families and friends suffer from the same social stigma. The diagnosis of AIDS may lead parents to realize for the first time that their son is homosexual. They confront imminent bereavement, suffering, and unnecessary shame in one devastating blow.

Furthermore, religious aspects can make the burden even heavier.

Religion and AIDS

In a television film I made in 1983 about people's attitudes to AIDS, we used some film of a leader of a fundamentalist church speaking (or rather, shouting) about AIDS. He was apoplectic with rage, and spoke of AIDS as the gay plague brought down by God to punish homosexuals for their sins. My immediate reaction to watching that preacher rant and rave was: "Would Jesus have said these things?"

The issue is an important one, because many AIDS victims are church members with strong religious convictions. Condemned by their own church, their deep pain is amplified as they are cut off from yet another source of comfort and sustenance. The fundamentalists are but one of the many Christian churches that recognize homosexuality as a sin. Therefore, in their vision, any homosexual is, by their definition, beyond the boundary of the church, and justly deserving of the retribution of God.

To me, the spectacle of the fundamentalist minister raging against AIDS was sickening. Here, I thought, was a Christian a long way away from the teaching of Christ. The principles of Christ's teachings are accessible to anyone, and are easy to understand. Jesus made a particular point of working among the people rejected by the society of his time. He went to the lepers, who were then feared and rejected more than AIDS victims today, he blessed prostitutes (including Mary Magdalen), and he protected the human rights of adulterers, about one of whom he said, "He that is without sin among you, let him first cast a stone." He taught forgiveness, tolerance, and charity. The only people with whom he became angry were the money-lenders in the Temple. Condemnation of those who suffered was no part of Christ's doctrine.

In fact, as I learned when we were discussing this particular issue, Christ had a particular point to make in the parable of the Good Samaritan. John Martin pointed out to me that in biblical times Samaritans had a very unattractive reputation. They were considered "the scum of the earth. They had about the same social standing as gypsies did under the Nazis. They were thought of as untrustworthy, unsavory, dishonest and dirty. Christ chose a Samaritan as the central figure of that parable because he wanted to say that it is a man's behavior that makes him a neighbor, not his social standing or the stratum of society he comes from. If Jesus was on earth today, he might easily have taken an AIDS carrier as the central figure of that parable: and He might have shown those people so prone to condemnation that AIDS carriers — like preachers, like doctors, like all human beings — are to be recognized by their behavior, their love and their charity. And not by the results of their blood tests."

In his daily work, John Martin often finds that he can be most useful, as a representative of the church, simply by standing by an AIDS patient and his partner, and by showing that they are not being abandoned. One couple said to me (of John's counseling and support), "I think we were expecting to be condemned or at least lectured — that's often the way it is these days. It was such an immense relief just to be listened to, and to have the feeling that someone in the church understood how awful we both feel."

What we all need to do, then, for AIDS patients is to *undo* the damage that bigotry, fear, ignorance, prejudice, and hate have already done. If you are helping and supporting a person with AIDS and are experiencing difficulty communicating easily with them, concentrate on treating that person as you would any other terminally ill patient. If you can ask yourself, "How would I behave if this person was dying of something other than AIDS?" then you have begun to counteract the social pressures surrounding you.

DISEASES INVOLVING LOSS OF MENTAL FUNCTION

Another medical problem that seems to set its victims apart from the rest of society is loss of mental function, or "dementia." Loss of mental ability can accompany many diseases of the brain and nervous system, including Alzheimer's disease, Huntington's chorea, and advanced stages of multiple sclerosis. There are special difficulties in such situations. The person who was previously loved and appreciated by friends and family disappears, replaced by a forgetful, irritable, unintelligible ghost who *looks* physically like the person everyone knew. The family may get angry and frustrated, and then in spite of the fact that theirs is the normal reaction, feel guilty about their anger. If this happens to you, you may find yourself trying to compensate for your imagined negligence by setting greater goals of help and support. If you cannot meet these more stringent demands, you may further increase your feelings of guilt.

Two different forces may be occupying your mind. On the one hand, if the dementia is advanced, you know that this human being is irrational and disoriented, and that it is no use trying to reason with him or insisting that he remember what you say. On the other hand, physically the person is still your father or mother or friend, and his appearance triggers your past emotional investment and gets reflex responses from you.

If you have not already done so, read the section in Chapter 11 on Losing a Parent, which gives you a logical structure to assess and plan a person's needs. In addition to the points I have made there, I would stress the additional demands made on the supporter when the patient is not rational. The supporter's task is difficult, because it calls for tolerance and evenness of temper while at the same time requiring the awareness that the person you knew is "not there." You need to detach yourself enough emotionally to protect yourself from desperate frustration, while simultaneously staying close enough to care for your friend physically. This hard and wearying task may bring you to the point at which you think you simply cannot cope. If that happens, it is very important that you think in detail about the other resources available to help you support the patient. Other members of the family, other social services, and other resources may be of value to you. Many self-help groups are useful in this context. They provide a forum for the supporter to ventilate the frustrations of caring for a person with dementia. They may not alter the physical and psychological pressures on you, but by allowing you to blow off steam, they may reduce the impact of these pressures on your own life.

Another critical point in the course of a person's dementing illness arises when she can no longer be cared for at home. There may well come a stage at which you and your family can no longer bear the strain of caring for a demented relative. It would be quite normal to then find an institution for her. This almost always makes the family feel even more guilty. You may feel that, if the patient is being institutionalized because the family can't take care of him anymore, you have failed. This is not so. There is a limit to what any family, any human being for that matter, can tolerate without asking for help. If it is necessary to save the mental health of your family by having the person with dementia be cared for elsewhere, it is a necessary step that does not imply that you have failed as a son or daughter. Mary faced this problem with her mother. Mary is a remarkably capable and competent woman — articulate, successful, and compassionate. However, it got to the point where she could no longer function normally. She found she was shouting at her husband, unkind to her children, unable to meet her deadlines (she was a journalist), and incapable of producing work that was, in her opinion, worthy of her. Her mother was at this stage totally unaware of who was looking after her and of anything that was going on. You might be thinking that it should have been very simple for Mary to get her mother admitted to an institution — and, in her heart, Mary knew it was the only viable option. Yet under the immense stress of the situation, Mary was surprised by how difficult it was. No matter how carefully she rationalized it, no matter how caringly she discussed it with her husband, it hurt her deeply to have her mother transferred to an institution. For a few weeks afterward, despite the relief and her family's return to normal life, Mary felt as if she had failed. As that pain faded, she came to realize that you can only do your best, and your best is all you can do.

In summary, every *person* is different, and every person suffering from a disease is special, even if thousands of others have the same disease. The common strand running through all these examples is the way in which you — the friends and family of the patient — can recognize what is going on, and the ways in which you can offer help.

13

Talking with
Health Professionals

The most common cause of patients' or relatives' dissatisfaction with the care provided is a gap in communication. While some complaints about the standard of doctors' communication are justified, on some occasions the patient or relative has not expressed his wishes clearly. In most cases, both parties must share some blame. Communications may just get off on the wrong foot. In this chapter I offer a simple checklist that can help you get the most out of your discussions with your friend's doctors or nurses. It may not turn a disagreement into peace and harmony, but it will at least ensure that you get your part right.

Doctors and nurses are only part of the team, but they are usually the gatekeepers and you need to get them to understand your friend's needs, so that the right auxiliary services can be called in. These services may include visiting nurses, social workers, counselors, chaplains, occupational therapists, physiotherapists, psychotherapists, psychiatrists, home care teams, and palliative care unit teams. In situations where the right help isn't reaching the patient, the most common problem is a communication gap. Either the doctors looking after the overall care of the patient aren't aware of the patient's particular needs, or the patient and friends aren't aware of what they can ask for.

Here is a simple scheme to help you maximize your chance of communicating effectively:

1. *Decide What Kind of Conversation You Want to Have.* Think clearly about what you want to say. There are really only four major types of conversation.

a. You want information from the doctor about the disease, treatment, or prognosis, either for your benefit or to clarify matters for the patient.

b. You want to give information about the patient's state or needs to the doctor or nurse.

c. You want to request additional services, support, or treatment for the patient.

d. You want support for yourself — to unburden yourself or get help.

Decide before you start which of these elements are on your agenda. It may be helpful to write them down for yourself (though it may be advisable not to have the list in front of you when you talk — some doctors react badly to written lists unless they have previously invited you to draw one up).

2. *Determine the Urgency of the Conversation.* Tell the doctor, nurse, or secretary whether or not you need to talk urgently. Sudden and dramatic changes in your friend's condition are urgent and you should call the hospital nurse

or emergency services or (if the situation does not quite qualify as an emergency) the family doctor. But for all other conversations with a doctor, give some indication of the priority. If your normal line of communication to the doctor is through a nurse, write down your name and number on a piece of paper. One of the most common causes of communication gaps is that someone forgets to deliver a message because he is busy.

You should also give some indication of how long you think you will need — a conversation of fifteen or twenty minutes can accomplish a great deal and is not an unreasonable demand.

3. *Consider Talking over the Phone.* Many doctors are better at talking over the phone (for they may feel less threatened), particularly if you have already met face to face. Consider whether what you have to say can be discussed over the phone. If so, try that first. It may be quicker and easier for both of you.

4. *Be Specific.* Try not to meander (although this happens often when people are nervous or under pressure of time). Come to the point as quickly as you can, and, bearing in mind the four kinds of conversation mentioned above, try to state each point in a way that calls for a specific response from the doctor or nurse.

5. *Expect Some Uncertainty.* Sadly, many questions — and often the most important ones — cannot be answered easily. In particular, questions about the future — no matter how well posed, no matter how willing the doctor is to try to answer — are often unanswerable. The doctor's responses may lack useful precision. He is usually not hedging, instead simply stating the way things are. Be prepared to accept uncertainty, however painful it is.

6. *Get Updated*. Put in a quick call to the ward on days when you cannot visit. Getting news in small daily pieces is preferable to visiting after a few days and finding that the situation has changed dramatically (with all the alarm and anxiety that may cause you).

7. *If You Are Dissatisfied, Pause*. It is very easy to direct your anger about the disease toward the doctors and nurses. If you think the doctors or nurses are providing unsatisfactory care, ask yourself whether you might actually be angry at the disease. Blaming the bearer for the bad news is a common reaction, one to watch for when you complain. Give yourself a little time to think before you take action. If you are sure that the care is unsatisfactory, tell the nurse in as cool and factual a manner as you can. If you still do not get satisfaction, speak to the doctor and then consider (after a further period of time) speaking to the hospital ombudsman, patient representative, patient advocate, or administrator. Do not do this unless you really have to, as it introduces an atmosphere of adversarial conflict into patient care which makes even simple communications more complex.

8. *Give Credit for a Good Job*. Doctors and nurses enter the health professions because they want to help people, and they like being told that they have done a good job. An appreciative note (if they deserve it) makes their day — and reinforces good supportive behavior in the doctor or nurse for the next patient. Even doctors are human.

Conclusion

🐝   I hope that I've shown you in this book some ways of approaching a situation which may have once appeared unapproachable. Perhaps I've given you some footsteps in the snow. You may or may not follow them — certainly there is no single and unique One True Path — but at least you now have the idea that you can do something, whereas previously you may have been unable to do anything because you thought nothing could be done. You may have been unable to say anything because you didn't know anything could be said.

I distrust simplicity, and don't believe that great truths can be boiled down into aphorisms on bumper stickers and T-shirts. I would say, however, that you are facing an abnormal situation. It's not your fault and it's not your friend's fault. In order to help in the best possible way, try to be normal. Try to talk normally and behave as normally as you can, but at the same time be a *little* more considerate, a little bit more sensitive, and a little bit kinder.

Above all, remember that, however frustrating it is,

however painful and difficult, and however exhausting, *supporting someone who is dying is one of the most valuable and worthwhile things that one human being can do for another*. I hope that this book has helped you to help others.

Appendix B

Supporting Organizations

SELF-HELP GROUPS

There are many self-help groups throughout the United Kingdom, composed of people working together to help others cope with the same illnesses or problems that they themselves have experienced first hand, be it specific diseases, bereavement, or widowhood. For information on self-help groups, contact:

> National Self-Help Support Centre
> 26 Bedford Square
> London
> WC1B 3HU

OTHER ORGANIZATIONS

British Voluntary
  Euthanasia Society
13 Prince of Wales Terrace
London W8 5PG
01-937-7770

Hospice Information Service
St Christopher's Hospice
51—59 Lawrie Park Rd
London SE26 6DZ
01-778-9252

The Hospice Information Service publishes a directory of the hospices throughout the UK. It also lists all other services available to help patients with cancer or amyotrophic lateral sclerosis.

Reverend Francis O'Leary
Jospice International
St Joseph's Hospice Association
Ince Road
Thorton
Liverpool L23 4UE

Hospices for the terminally ill and those ill but treatable with no one to care for them in Liverpool, England; Pakistan; Colombia; Peru; Ecuador; Honduras; Guatemala.

Cancer Relief Macmillan Fund
Anchor House
15—19 Britten Street
London SW3 3TZ
01-351-7811

Provides support for all cancer patients.

Marie Curie Cancercare   Cancerlink
28 Belgrave Square   46 Pentonville Road
London SW1X 8QG   London
                                      N1 9HF
                                      01-833-2451

Cancerlink is a national organization offering two services: information and support about all aspects of cancer for patients and their families and friends, as well as a group support service linking up self-help groups throughout Britain.

BACUP
British Association of Cancer United Patients
121–123 Charterhouse Street
London EC1M 6AA
01-608-1661

BACUP offers a national cancer information service with oncology nurses as well as a counselling service with volunteers who provide support for all aspects of cancer and bereavement and can direct callers to a wide variety of community resources.

World Federation of Right to Die Societies
c/o Association pour le droit de mourir dans la dignité (ADMD)
103 rue la Fayette
75010 Paris, France

Recommended Reading

BOOKS WITH SPECIFIC ADVICE

Carroll, David. *Living with Dying*. McGraw-Hill, 1985.

Grollman, Earl. *Explaining Death to Children*. Beacon Press, 1967.

Myers, Edward. *When Parents Die*. Penguin Books, 1987.

Schiff, Harriet Sarnott. *The Bereaved Parent*. Crown Publishing, 1977.

Wylie, Betty Jane. *Beginnings: A Book for Widows*. McClelland and Stewart, 1985.

BOOKS OF GENERAL INTEREST

Becker, Ernest. *The Denial of Death*. Macmillan, 1973.

Glaser, Barney, and Anselm Strauss. *Awareness of Dying*. Aldine Publishing, 1965.

Harpur, Tom. *For Christ's Sake*. Oxford University Press, 1986.

Hinton, John. *Dying*. Penguin Books, 1967.

Kübler-Ross, Elisabeth. *On Death and Dying*. Tavistock Publications, 1970.

Pincus, Lily. *Death and the Family: The Importance of Mourning*. Faber, 1974.

Rando, Theresa. *Grief, Dying and Death*. Research Press Company, 1984.

Worden, J. William. *Grief Counseling and Grief Therapy*. Springer, 1982.

FOR FURTHER INFORMATION

Compassionate Book Service
208 Montgomery Avenue
Ann Arbor, MI 48103
313-665-8358

This firm specializes in books on death, grief, comfort, and hope. It has an excellent catalogue of approximately two hundred books available on request.

Index

abandonment
    child's experience of, after death of
        parent, 204, 206, 207, 213
    dying alone and, 129
    fear of, 90
acceptance, of inevitability of death,
    108–109
    differences in, between patient and
        friends or relatives, 114–115
    medical facts and, 116–119
achievements, fears related to, 60–61
advice, offering too early, 27
afterlife images, 110, 145, 213
AIDS, 50, 183, 214–219
    homophobia and, 215–216
    mysticism and divine retribution
        linked to, 216–217
    religious beliefs and, 217–219
    transmission of, 214–215
alternative medicines, 114–115, 119–
    121
    anger after failure of, 120
    common traits of, 119–120
    practical points to check about,
        121

anger:
    alternative medicines and, 120
    in "being ill" stage, 102–103
    in child after death of parent,
        213
    expressions of, 107
    in "facing the threat" stage, 54–
        59, 74–77
    at fate or God, 56, 57
    friends and relatives as targets of,
        32–33, 83–84
    friends' and relatives' experience
        of, 74–77, 102–103
    at people who are trying to help,
        56, 57–59
    powerlessness as cause of, 55
    sexual problems and, 183
    "why me?" 55, 56–57
anticipatory grief, 103, 136, 141–
    142
antidepressants, 63
anxiety, 48
    talking and, 18
arguments, escalation of, 32–34
atmosphere, for conversations, 22–23

bargaining, 65–66
bed-wetting, after death of parent,
    209
"being ill" stage, 38, 91–107
    anger in, 102–103
    choices and decisions in, 104–106
    denial in, 92
    depression in, 92
    despair in, 91
    emotional impact of physical
        symptoms in, 96–101
    friends' and relatives' feelings in,
        101–103
    "grind" in, 93–95
    hope in, 91
    patient's feelings in, 92–101
    physical illness in, 92–93
    practical needs in, 104
    support in, 95, 103–107
    sympathetic feelings in, 101–102
    "what's the point?" feeling in, 99–
        100
bereavement counseling, 144, 210
blame:
    for death of child, 195
    placed on patient for illness, 77–78
    societal emphasis on, 66–67
breast surgery:
    emotional impact of, 96–98
    sex drive after, 182
brother, death of, 188–190, 198, 213

cancer organizations, 232
cardiac resuscitation, 125
cervical cancer, contagion fears and,
    183
checklist for offering help, 159–163
chemotherapy, hair loss due to, 98,
    104
child, death of, 191–204
    asking for help after, 204
    avoiding big decisions after, 203
    bereavement period after, 202–
        204
    blame for, 195
    books about, 202

clinging to child's objects after,
    202–203
divorce after, 195, 204
finding out what is best for your
    child in, 198
finding out what your child
    understands in, 196–197
getting informed about child's
    disease in, 196
idealization of child after, 202, 213
involving other family members in,
    198–199
list of resources in, 197–198
maintaining normal life during,
    199
parent's reaction to, 194–196
practical plans in, 196–199
responsibility bonds and, 194
sharing grief selectively after, 203
talking and listening during, 199–
    202
children:
    activities refused by, 205
    anger experienced by, 213
    concentration span of, 200
    consistency important to, 208–209
    death of parent and, 82, 204–213
    extreme responses of, 206
    finding out what's going on with,
        209
    getting help with, 210
    guilt feelings of, 82, 204–205, 207,
        211
    hospital visits of, 206
    including in activities, 206
    making time for, 209
    planning future for, 178–179
    regressive behavior in, 209
    reminiscence about dead parent
        important for, 211–212
    reserving time for, 207
    role of dead parent filled by, 210–
        211
    school performance and, 206–207,
        209
    sharing grief with, 212–213

sibling's death and, 198, 213
talking and listening to, 211–213
understanding of death in, at
    different ages, 192–193
colostomy:
emotional impact of, 98
sexual problems after, 181, 182
coma, in dying process, 111, 128
communication:
nonverbal, 24–25
obstacles to, 19
styles of, 20–21
talking as best method of, 16
See also conversations; listening;
    talking
contagion, fear of, 183
control, loss of:
anger caused by, 55
friends' and relatives' experience
    of, 113–114
over physical symptoms, 99
conversations:
changing subject in, 27
describing your own feelings in,
    25–26
encouraging patient to talk in, 24
eye contact in, 23
finding out whether patient wants
    to talk before, 23
interruptions in, 24
making sure you haven't
    misunderstood in, 26
offering advice in, 27
physical context of, 22–23
physical distance between
    participants in, 23
reminiscence encouraged in, 27–
    28
responding to humor in, 28–29
showing that you're listening in,
    23–24
silence and nonverbal
    communication in, 24–25
styles of communication in, 20–21
See also communication; listening;
    talking

coping abilities, recovered memories
    and, 28
crying:
in initial phase of grief, 134–136
other people's objections to, 135

death:
accepting inevitability of, 108–109,
    114–115, 116–119
of child, 191–204
child's understanding of, 192–193
denial of, 6–7
facing threat of, 38, 42–90 See
    also "facing the threat" stage
of friend, 190–191
isolated from mainstream of life,
    6–11
of parent, 164–174
of sibling, 188–190, 198, 213
of spouse, 174–188
See also dying
decision-making:
breakdown in, as symptom of
    shock, 44
after death of child, 203
after death of spouse, 187
helping patient with, 104–106
dementia, 219–222
difficulties in providing support
    for, 220–221
institutionalization for, 221–222
denial, 177, 190
in "being ill" stage, 92
as conflict between knowledge and
    belief, 46
of death, 6–7
disappearance of, 109
disbelief vs., 45
distress caused by, 49, 51–54
in "facing the threat" stage, 45–
    54, 86–87
in friends and relatives, 73–74
friends and relatives as targets of,
    83
helping with, 86–88
medical needs and, 49–51

denial (continued)
  and need to face facts, 47–48, 49–51, 54
  planning hindered by, 51
  power of, 46–47
  refusing surgery as, 106
  shopping around for medical treatments as, 118
  withholding of information and, 48–49
depression, 48
  in "being ill" stage, 92
  in "facing the threat" stage, 63–64
  physical signs of, 63
  sexual appetite decreased by, 182
  talking and, 18
  treatment of, 63–64
despair:
  bargaining as battle between hope and, 65–66
  in "being ill" stage, 91
  cyclical nature of, 62–63
  expressions of, 107
  in "facing the threat" stage, 61–63, 89–90
  friends and relatives as targets of, 83
  helping with, 89–90
diagnosis, responses to, 42–43 See also "facing the threat" stage
disbelief:
  denial vs., 45
  in "facing the threat" stage, 43–44
  in friends and relatives, 73
divorce, after death of child, 195, 204
doctors:
  anger at, 56, 58
  patient's relationship with, 118–119
  reluctant to accept failure of their techniques, 9
  talking with, 223–226
  trained in care at end of life, 9
  See also medical treatments
Doll's House, A, 216

dying, 35–156
  fear of, 59, 60, 106
  friends and relatives absent at moment of, 128–130
  at home, 7–8, 122
  medical facts about, 111, 128
  near-dying experiences and, 111–112
  as province of experts, 8–10
  similarity between way of living and, 110–111, 112
  transition in, 37–41
  See also "being ill" stage; death; "facing the threat" stage; last stage

emotions:
  feeling several at same time, 39–40
  See also specific emotions
endorphins, 112
euthanasia, 130–131
exhaustion, in friends and relatives, 113
existential fears, 60
eye contact, in conversations, 23

"facing the threat" stage, 38, 42–90
  anger in, 54–59, 74–77
  denial in, 45–54, 86–88
  depression in, 63–64
  despair in, 61–63, 89–90
  fears in, 59–61, 78–80
  friends' and relatives' feelings in, 70–84
  guilt in, 66–70, 80–82
  hope in, 62, 64–66, 87, 89, 90
  patient's feelings in, 43–70
  shock and disbelief in, 43–45, 62
  support during, 84–90
false hopes, 62, 64–65, 89
Families — And How to Survive Them, 171
fate, anger at, 56, 57
fears:
  of abandonment, 90
  of being afraid, 59–60

of catching partner's disease, 183
childhood, after bereavement, 209
of dying, 59, 60, 106
existential, 60
expressions of, 106
in "facing the threat" stage, 59–61,
    78–80
in friends and relatives, 78–80
imagination required for, 60
life achievements and, 60–61
of physical pain, 60
practical, 61
talking and, 18, 61
finances, death of spouse and, 178
forgetfulness, as symptom of shock,
    44
forgetting, as concern of patient,
    126–127
Fosse, Bob, 124
Frayn, Michael, 91
friend, death of, 190–191
friends and relatives:
    absent at moment of death, 128–
        130
    acceptance differences in, 114–115
    anger directed at, 32–33, 83–84
    anger experienced by, 74–77, 102–
        103
    denial in, 73–74
    emotional and physical exhaustion
        in, 113
    fears of, 78–80
    feelings of, as observers, 71, 72–
        82, 102–103
    feelings of, as "targets," 71, 82–84
    feelings of, in "being ill" stage,
        101–103
    feelings of, in "facing the threat"
        stage, 70–84
    feelings of, in last stage, 112–115
    guilt felt by, 80–82
    loss of control experienced by,
        113–114
    patient blamed for illness by, 77–
        78
    resentment felt by, 102–103

shock and disbelief felt by, 73
sympathetic feelings of, 71, 72,
    101–102
fundamentalism, AIDS and, 217–218
future, telescoping of, 69–70

Ghosts, 216
God, 10, 145, 146
    AIDS and, 216, 217, 218–219
    anger at, 56, 57
    bargaining between patient and,
        65
    praying to, 149–151
    "why me?" question directed to,
        147–149
Good Samaritan, parable of, 218
Great Britain, narcotic painkillers in,
    131
Great Expectations, 133
grief, 132–144
    anticipatory, 103, 136, 141–142
    crying in, 134–136
    after death of child, 202–204
    after death of spouse, 186–188
    function of, 132–133
    initial stage of, 134–136
    middle stage of, 136–139
    outsiders' discomfort with, 135,
        138
    pathological, 142–144
    in patient, 110
    physical symptoms of, 136
    questioning aspects of past in,
        138–139
    resentment in, 139
    resolution phase of, 139–141
    semblance of normality and, 136–
        137
    sharing with children, 212–213
    timetables for, 140–141
    unrealistic expectations about,
        137–138
guilt, 179
    anticipatory grief and, 141–142
    and association of patient's
        behavior with disease, 67, 68–69

guilt (*continued*)
  capitalizing on inherent sense of,
    69
  in child after death of parent, 204–
    205, 207, 211
  in child after death of sibling, 213
  for death of child, 194
  in "facing the threat" stage, 66–
    70, 80–82
  in family of demented patient, 220,
    221
  friends and relatives as targets of,
    83
  friends' and relatives' feelings of,
    80–82
  large gifts due to, 162
  personal responsibility and, 66–67
  reward and punishment ideas and,
    66, 67–68, 80
  sensitivity as requirement for, 70
  sexual problems and, 183–184, 185
  survivor, 82, 133
  about unfinished business, 69–70

hair loss, 98, 104
health care. *See* medical treatments
health professionals:
  talking with, 223–226
  See also doctors; nurses
Holland, euthanasia in, 130–131
home, dying at, 7–8, 122
homophobia, 215–216
homosexuals:
  AIDS among, 215–219
  religious beliefs and, 217–219
hope, 120, 177
  bargaining as battle between
    despair and, 65–66
  in "being ill" stage, 91
  in "facing the threat" stage, 62,
    64–66, 87, 89–90
  false, 62, 64–65, 89
  of miracles, 64–65
  realistic, reinforcing of, 90, 100
hospices, 122–123, 131
hospital visits by children, 206

humor:
  as cure for physical illnesses, 29–
    30
  responding to, 28–29

Ibsen, Henrik, 216
idealization, of child who has died,
  202, 213
illness:
  getting informed about, 47–51,
    160, 167, 175–176, 196
  humor or laughter as cure for, 29–
    30
  patient blamed for, 77–78
  patient's behavior associated with,
    67, 68–69
  patient's physical condition in, 92–
    93
  as retribution, 67–68
  See also "being ill" stage
immortality, 11
impatience, in friends and relatives,
  113
information:
  on child's disease, 196
  helper's need for, 86, 160
  on parent's disease, 167
  patient's need for, 47–48, 49–51
  on spouse's disease, 175–176
  withholding from patient, 48–49
institutionalization, of demented
  patient, 221–222
interruptions, in conversations with
  patient, 24
isolation, 18, 48
  of death from mainstream of life,
    6–11

King Henry IV (Part 2), 141
Kübler-Ross, Elisabeth, 39

last rites, 115
last stage, 38, 108–131
  accepting inevitability of death in,
    108–109, 114–115, 116–119
  alternative medicines in, 119–121

being forgotten as concern in, 126–127

demands you cannot meet in, 127–128

friends' and relatives' feelings in, 112–115

helping patient after acceptance in, 121–131

helping patient before acceptance in, 116–121

last wishes in, 122–124

living wills and, 124–125, 131, 229

medical facts established in , 116–119

patient's feelings in, 109–112

practicalities in, 121–125

laughter, as cure for physical illnesses, 29–30

life achievements, fears related to, 60–61

listening, 20–30, 162

atmosphere for talking created by, 21

to child after loss parent, 211–213

to dying child, 199–202

to dying parent, 170–173

effectiveness of, 17

responses to patient during, 24, 25–26

and showing that you're listening, 23–24

See also conversations; talking

Livingstone, David, 112

living wills, 124–125, 131

sample of, 229

loss, impending sense of, 71–72, 73, 82, 103

malaise, 94–95

marriage:

within last few days of life, 124

strained by death of child, 195, 196, 204

See also spouse, death of

mastectomy. See breast surgery

masturbation, 185

materialism, 10, 11

medical facts, establishing of, 116–119

medical treatments:

advances in, 8

alternative, 119–121

high-tech, 8–9

living wills and, 124–125, 131, 229

patient's freedom of choice in, 104–106

patient's need for information in, 49–51

second opinions and, 117–118

side effects of, 104, 105

memories. See reminiscences

mental function, diseases involving loss of. See dementia

Middlemarch, 127

miracles

hopes of, 64–65

praying for, 151

misunderstandings, 26

mood swings, 62–63, 85

mortality, intimations of, 190

mourning:

by patient, 110

See also grief

narcotic painkillers, 131

near-dying experiences, 111–112

needs, assessing of, 160–161

in "being ill" stage, 104

in death of parent, 168

in death of spouse, 176–177, 187

nonverbal communication, 24–25

normal life:

maintaining of, during death of child, 199

semblance of, in grieving process, 136–137

nurses:

anger at, 56, 58

talking with, 223–226

pain:

fears about, 60

humor in raising threshold of, 29–30
narcotics in relief of, 131
relief from, as realistic hope, 90
sexual appetite decreased by, 182
"what's the point?" question and, 99–100
painkillers, 131
palliative care units, 122–123, 131
parent, death of, 164–174
    assessing needs in, 168
    awkwardness of support role in, 165–166
    flexibility and changeability of plans in, 170
    getting informed about parent's disease in, 167
    guide to making plans for, 167–170
    listening and talking in, 170–173
    list of resources for, 169
    painfulness of, 164–165
    plans for children in, 178–179
    range of future scenarios in, 167
    small realistic plans in, 170
    son's vs. daughter's response to, 166
    trying to find out what parent wants in, 168–169
    vulnerability experienced after, 165
    "what if ..." plans in, 169–170
    young child's response to, 204–213
parents:
    child's relationship with, 170-172
    reactions of, to dying child, 194–196
See also child, death of
physical symptoms:
    emotional impact of, 96–101
    of grief, 136
    as "grind," 93–95
    individual priorities and, 96
    patient's lack of control over, 99
    progression of, 92–93
    of shock, 44–45

planning:
    during death of child, 196–199
    during death of parent, 167–170
    during death of spouse, 175–180
    flexibility and changeability in, 170, 180
    hindered by denial, 51
    range of future scenarios and, 167
    "what if ...," 167–170, 177
    for worst while hoping for best, 65
powerlessness:
    anger caused by, 55
    friends' and relatives' experience of, 113–114
    over physical symptoms, 99
prayer, 149–151
    miracles requested in, 151
    therapeutic benefits of, 150–151
promises, to patient, 89, 90, 127–128
punishment. See reward and punishment

questions, in middle stage of grief, 138–139

relatives. See friends and relatives
religious beliefs, 110, 145–156
    afterlife images and, 110, 145, 213
    AIDS and, 217–219
    "bad" theology and, 152–154
    changes in, 10
    differences in, 154–155
    "good" theology and, 146
    prayer and, 149–151
    "why me?" question and, 147–149
reminiscences:
    about dead parent, 211–212
    encouraging of, 27–28
    sibling relationship and, 189–190
repetition, 86
resentment:
    in friends and relatives, 102–103
    in grieving process, 139
resources, making list of, 206
    for death of child, 197–198
    for death of parent, 169

for death of spouse, 177–178, 187
responsibility:
    death of child and, 194
    guilt and, 66–67
    resuscitation, cardiac, 125
reward and punishment:
    in "bad" theology, 152–154, 156
    guilt and, 66, 67–68, 80

sadness:
    about impending loss, 73
    in initial phase of grief, 134
    in last stage, 109–110
school:
    notifying of death of parent, 206–207
    watching for behavioral changes at, 209
second opinions, 117–118
self-help groups, 231
sexual problems, 180–186
    and being specific about what you can do, 184–186
    emotional factors in, 182–183
    getting help for, 186
    guilt and, 183–184, 185
    partner's changed appearance and, 184, 185
    physical causes of, 181–182
    prevalence of, among ill people, 180
    privacy requests and, 186
    sleeping in same vs. different bed and, 186
    talking about, 184
Shakespeare, William, 141
shame, bottled up feelings as cause of, 18
shock:
    in "facing the threat" stage, 43–45, 62
    friends' and relatives' experience of, 73
    in initial phase of grief, 134, 136
    symptoms of, 44–45
sibling, death of, 188–190

appropriate role in, 189
child's experience of, 198, 213
vulnerability experienced in, 188–189
side effects, 104, 105
silence, 24–25
sister, death of, 188–190, 198, 213
Skynner, Robin, 171
sleep problems, in children, 209
slowness, as symptom of shock, 44
spiritual aspects, 10, 145–156
    support in, 155–156
    See also religious beliefs
spouse, death of, 174–188
    bereavement period after, 186–188
    estimating future needs in, 176–177
    flexibility of plans in, 180
    getting clear idea of what each of you wants in, 177
    getting informed about spouse's disease in, 175–176
    guide to making plans for, 175–180
    making list of resources in, 177–178
    planning future for all family members in, 178–179
    sexual problems and, 180–186
    sleeping in same vs. different bed and, 186
    stunted emotional growth after, 144
    thinking about your past relationship during, 176
stupor, in dying process, 128
suicide, 135
support:
    activity vs., 86
    assessing needs in, 104, 160–161, 168, 176–177 187
    avoiding excesses in, 162
    during "being ill" stage, 95, 103–107
    checklist for, 159–163

support (*continued*)
of child after death of parent, 208, 213
deciding what you can and want to do in, 161
dementia and, 220–221
of dying child, 196–199
of dying parent, 165–166, 167–174
of dying spouse, 175–180
exploring what patient really wants and means in, 106–107
during "facing the threat" stage, 84–90
flexibility and changeability of plans in, 170, 180
general guidelines for, 85–86
getting clear idea what each of you wants in, 177
getting informed in, 86, 160, 167, 175–176, 196
helping patient make choices in, 104–106
helping with denial, 86–88
helping with despair, 89–90
involving other people in, 161–62
in last stage, 116–131
list of resources in, 169, 177–178, 187, 197–198, 206
making your offer for, 159–160
mood swings and, 85
patient's agenda in, 86
range of future scenarios and, 167
repetition and, 86
seeing where you fit in, 85
in spiritual understanding of death, 155–156
starting with small, practical things in, 161–162
trying to find out what patient wants and, 168–169
"what if ..." plans in, 169–170, 177
See also listening
supporting organizations, 231–233
cancer organizations, 232
self-help groups, 231

survivor guilt, 82, 133
sympathetic feelings:
in "being ill" stage, 101–102
in "facing the threat" stage, 71, 72
symptoms. *See* physical symptoms
syphilis, 216

talking, 15–19
as best method of communication, 16
with child after loss of parent, 211–213
distress relieved by, 16–17
with dying child, 199–202
with dying parent, 170–173
fears or anxieties and, 18, 61
with health professionals, 223–226
patient's desires for, 23
about sexual problems, 184
See also conversations; listening
teenagers, seriously ill, 193
transition, 37–41
feeling several emotions at same time in, 39–40
three stages in, 38–39 *See also* "being ill" stage; "facing the threat" stage; last stage
uncertainty at strain in, 41
unusual reactions in, 42–43
variability in patterns of, 40–41
transitional objects, 202–203
tumors, contagion fears and, 183

uncertainty, 225
difficulty of living with, 41, 91
unfinished business, guilt about, 69–70

vulnerability:
parent's death and, 165
sibling's death and, 188–189

wakes, arranged by dying patient, 123–124
wellness, in early part of illness, 93
"what if ..." plans, 169–170, 177

"what's the point?" feeling, 99–100

"why me?" anger, 55, 56–57

"why me, God?" question, 147–149

wills, 122

living, 124–125, 131, 229

wishes, last, 122–124, 127–128

words-repetition technique, 24

World Federation of Right to Die Societies, 232